Traditional Homes of the South Downs National Park

Traditional Homes of the South Downs National Park

An Introduction

by Annabelle Hughes

ISBN 978-0-904973-26-6

Published by the Sussex Archaeological Society, Lewes

Printed in Great Britain by Short Run Press, Exeter

Contents

The market hall in Midhurst

Acknowledgements

My thanks must go to the editorial team of Robin Milner-Gulland and John Manley. I am also grateful to John Manley for providing many photographs for the book. Other photographs are from my own (archive) collection, so taken from a practical point of view, rather than with artistry in mind. Those of Chesil Rectory and the Red Lion at Chalton were kindly supplied by the occupants. Any maps are used with the permission of the West Sussex Record Office. Jan Newbury kindly proof-read the text. For drawings my gratitude to Mary Mahler, to the memory of Margaret Goodare and to Ptolemy Dean, who shares my passion for buildings.

Dr Annabelle Hughes

This cottage at Steyning is only a small part of the original building, which probably dated from the transitional period (1500s).

Foreword

There were many of us who were delighted by the designation of the South Downs as a National Park. But the National Park extends some way northwards beyond the magnificent chalky southern downland landscape into the intimate and heavily wooded areas of the High Weald. Here flint gives way to oak timbering and sandstone in edible-looking shades of caramel and brown.

It was this geology that determined the patterns of land use, and the Wealden clay that made movement across large parts of this area so difficult. In a way it was this intractability that has helped to protect what is now the National Park from excess development in the past. Even today, the cross-country A272 is very much easier to drive along its western sections over the downland chalk, than along its contorted and winding eastern sections, where the Wealden clay geology has forced a seemingly perverse and tortured route. This geology has in turn shaped the character and location of villages and towns, and the layout and character of the farm landscape. The houses simply reflect the materials that surrounded them in built form. It is this rich diversity of materials that makes the buildings selected by Annabelle so visually appealing. But this is only half of the story.

What makes these buildings historically interesting is the very much deeper understanding of the historic and economic culture that has produced them gradually over many centuries. This is not so easily read from buildings alone, but requires careful research through the archives. It is here that Annabelle's highly refined sense of understanding has enabled her to ferret her way through the County Record Offices. Dusty bundles of brown, semi-legible documents held in the archives can initially seem as intractable and difficult to penetrate as landscape itself. But they can be equally rewarding. Archive findings bring clear and enlightening explanation for both the very grand and also the very modest.

It is all too easy for any of us to admire what is visually impressive and accomplished. And without archive understanding, it can be less easy to understand how a shabby lean to or seemingly worthless out-shot might be just as significant as a great façade in explaining the whole story of a building and the succession of its owners. As the area covered by this book becomes increasingly wealthy and sought after, it is the humble and the ordinary that is becoming increasingly exceptional and rare. Out in the countryside, the old unconverted barns and shacks are easy prey for the 'must-have' kitchen extension or 'gym and leisure suite'. Of course these things are probably lovely to have, but all too often they come at the expense of the simple qualities of working buildings that made this area so hauntingly beautiful in the first instance. The authentic is increasingly giving way to the suburban.

For years it was the Wealden clay that had protected access to much of this special area. Now we must rely on the knowledge, wisdom and understanding of people like Annabelle, to explain the significance of the seemingly insignificant so that these things can be fully appreciated and valued. We must therefore hope that this book will help attract others to take up the challenge of delving more deeply into this remarkably well-endowed region.

Ptolemy Dean
Architect and Surveyor of the
Fabric at Westminster Abbey

*This book is arranged in several sections: there is **a continuous text** set out under headings, and within this a series of **information 'boxes'** on related subjects, which can be referred to independently. You may like to read through the continuous text ignoring the 'boxes' and go back to these later, or you can go through the text, stopping to read the 'boxes' on the way. This is followed by a section on documentary sources, with three case studies showing how these can be combined for a more detailed picture of the development of a house over time – in two cases with simple ground plans – and finally there is a section on **'house detecting'** from the outside, with suggestions on what to look for.*

The illustrations follow a similar pattern. Some (numbered) are referenced in the text, the others (unnumbered) are 'stand-alone' pictures with explanatory captions.

Traditional Homes in the South Downs National Park

Getting Started

Anyone visiting the South Downs National Park will see innumerable cottages and houses that are frequently described as *'quaint'* or *'picturesque'*, or more formally as *'vernacular architecture'*. This guide will concentrate on those that were built from the mid 1200s until about 1750 – generally the homes of the middle and lower ranks of society. By passing on some of the things I have learned in over 30 years examining buildings (primarily in West Sussex), making written records of their structures and researching their documentary histories, I hope to enable readers to go out and make their own discoveries; once you have got into the habit of really looking at buildings, you can see interesting ones almost anywhere. Hopefully you will become something of a 'house detective', even if most of the detecting will be done from the outside. If this inspires you to delve deeper, at the end of the book there are some suggestions of more specialist literature.

A guide like this cannot be a definitive history of buildings, but aims to help you to understand and appreciate those you can see throughout the South Downs National Park. It will explore some of the reasons for their existence, some of the ways in which they were constructed and altered and some of the details to look for. These are some of the questions you should always keep in mind:

- Why is this house where it is?
- How old is it?
- What did it look like when it was first built?
- What changes have been made?
- When could these changes have been made?
- Why were these changes made?

The word *'architecture'*, with all its implications of fine art and design, seems too grand a word to describe these houses. Before the middle of the 1700s ordinary people did not commission some professional to design their home on drawing boards in an office, but were driven by the need to build shelters for their families, just as they built hovels and barns for their livestock and grain. These were places of refuge and recuperation when the weather was too harsh or the days too short to work outside for long, and their forms were developed using traditional skills and by trial and error.

These houses were *'vernacular'* in the sense that they were put together from the materials that were easily available: timber frames with wattle panels daubed with mud and then covered with lime-wash; flint and stone rubble trimmed with local bricks; and all roofed with straw thatch or stone slabs or clay tiles fixed to battens with oak pegs. They were *'indigenous'*: they belonged to the locality; they appeared to grow out of the ground rather than being imposed upon it. *'The ground beneath your feet'* – the geology – influenced what natural materials were to hand, and human activity managed the way in which these materials were produced and used. A good look at the map of the geology of the area can discover the links between the land

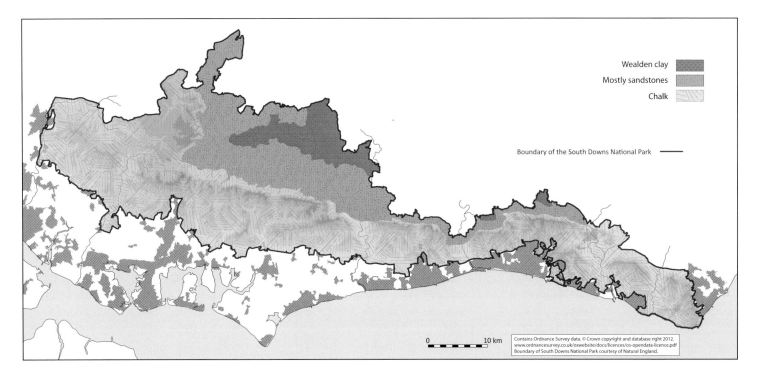

Wealden clay
Mostly sandstones
Chalk

Boundary of the South Downs National Park ——————

0   10 km

Contains Ordnance Survey data. © Crown copyright and database right 2012.
www.ordnancesurvey.co.uk/oswebsite/docs/licences/os-opendata-licence.pdf
Boundary of South Downs National Park courtesy of Natural England.

1. The geology of the area has influenced both where settlements were established and the materials used in house-building.

and early buildings, not only through the availability of building materials but also the kind of agricultural activity that could be supported and sustained in different areas **(1)**.

Houses cannot be fully understood in isolation from their topographical and historical settings, without losing something along the way. This is an attempt to place the buildings of the Park into their environmental and historical context. All along the northern slopes of the Downs spring-line settlements can be found that are apparently haphazard huddles of buildings gathered around a church, but there is often a pattern to be discovered, even if obscured by modern developments. For example, some such groups seem to have grown around an open 'green', possibly an informal market place or corporate 'dumping ground', others are strung along rural roads that might be the lines of old tracks, or clustered close to

2. A view of the village of Poynings, West Sussex, with the 14th century church in the foreground, and the settlement extending from it. This is a typical spring-line settlement just north of the Downs. The scarp face of the South Downs forms the horizon.

river crossings. These differences show up best on early maps **(2)**.

There are also farmsteads that are scattered a good walk away from both neighbours and Sunday worship, hidden in the folds of the Downs or tucked away in the Wealden woodland. Looking at maps, both old and new, and tracing footpaths are two ways to make the important links between houses and features that might explain the reasons for their location, such as access to water and the nearest markets.

For example, the bridge at Stopham, connecting the villagers of Sutton and further south with the market at Petworth, is first mentioned in 1279.

How villages look today can be deceptive. Although Amberley's history of ownership by the Bishops of Chichester goes back well before 1066, and it has a high proportion of thatched early buildings, only three of about twenty houses can be dated to before 1500. Over the river, Houghton is smaller and less impressive but was also owned by the bishops, and of its seven thatched houses, four date from the 1400s or earlier. It looks as though the tenants of Amberley were affluent enough to be able to replace most of their housing stock during the century after 1500, while those at Houghton were less affluent, and/or could only afford to update them. It also helps to know a bit of the history behind the buildings, and the list of monarchs and national events may jog the memory.

The medieval proportions of this house at Hardham, south of Pulborough, are easily recognisable. The long passing brace to the left is characteristic, and the narrower studs in the central bay (below the chimney) may be remnants of the window for a two-storey open hall. The brick bay to the right may be a later extension.

▶ The elevation of this house at Amberley shows some of the changes that have been made over the centuries.

KINGS & QUEENS of ENGLAND

Edward the Confessor	1042–66		Edward V	1483	*Died in the Tower*
Harold II	1066		Richard III	1483–85	*Killed in battle*
	Norman Conquest		Henry VII (Tudor)	1485–1509	
			Henry VIII	1509–47	
William I (Conqueror)	1066–87		*1539 Dissolution of monasteries*		
William II (Rufus)	1087–1100	*Killed while hunting*	Edward VI	1547–53	
Henry I	1100–35		Mary (m Philip of Spain)	1553–58	
Stephen	1135–54		Elizabeth I	1558–1603	
	Civil war (with Matilda)		*1588 Spanish Armada*		
Henry II (Beauclerk)	1154–89		James I (Stuart)	1603–25	
Richard I (Lionheart)	1189–1199		Charles I	1625–49	*Beheaded*
John (Lackland)	1199–1216		*Oliver Cromwell 1649–1660 Commonwealth*		
Henry III	1216–72		Charles II	1660–1685	
Edward I (Longshanks)	1272–1307		James II	1685–88	*Deposed*
Edward II	1307–27	*Purportedly died in prison*	William & Mary	1689–94	
	1315–22 The Great Famine		William (III)	1694–1702	
			Anne	1702–14	
Edward III	1327–77		George I (Hanover)	1714–27	
	1348/9 The Black Death		George II	1727–60	
Richard II	1377–99	*Died in prison*	George III	1760–1820	
	1381 The Peasants' Revolt		*1775–83 American Revolution*		
Henry IV	1399–1413		*1789–99 French Revolution*		
Henry V	1413–22		*Regency (from 1812)*		
Henry VI	1422–61	*Died in the Tower*			
	1450 Cade's Rebellion		George IV	1820–30	
	1455 Outbreak of civil war		William IV	1830–37	
Edward IV	1461–83		Victoria	1837–1901	

Buildings and building development can often be linked with national events and monarchical history.

1066 And All That

When the Normans invaded and Duke William seized the Crown, they did not find a blank canvas. Although England was predominantly a rural society, and the majority of its population was involved in agriculture, it was also a sophisticated, cultured nation state, with a well-organized and centralized administration, a stable currency and a fully developed taxation system. All this made England very attractive to William and his followers. Being chiefly military men, once they had side-lined those members of the English ruling classes who had not been killed at Hastings or gone into exile, they set about reorganising the existing systems of land-holding to secure their own future. This reorganization was based on the accepted fact that everything belonged to William, and through him to those he appointed directly to share responsibility. In turn, his tenants-in-chief rewarded (and attracted) their own followers with grants of land and property in return for economic and military support, and that practice went on down the line. Much property and large tracts of land were already in the hands of the Church (bishops and archbishops) and various other religious foundations (monasteries and nunneries, not all in England) and further gifts were made by the King and his followers, as insurance against what they believed might happen to them after death.

> *'William, king of the English, ordered all of the possessions of the whole of England to be described, in fields, in men, in all animals, in all manors from the greatest to the smallest, and in all payments which could be rendered from the land of all. And the land was vexed with much violence proceeding therefrom'*
>
> **Chronicle of Marianus Scotus from Worcester**

We have a unique record, if incomplete, both of England before 1066 and of the process of re-organisation by the Normans. A national survey was carried out 20 years after that battle near Hastings, at a time when England was once more under threat of invasion, this time from Denmark. Once the results were in his hands and before he left England for the last time, William summoned his leading subjects to Salisbury, to renew their oaths of loyalty. That threat came to nothing, and after William's death at the end of 1087, the results of the survey were edited and written up during the reign of his son, William Rufus, and eventually became known as the '**Domesday Book**'. As a 'book' it was notable in a period when records were more often kept on 'rolls'. Although there is nothing quite like it surviving anywhere else in Europe, it can be very frustrating: much of what it tells us we don't understand, and it doesn't tell us many things we would like to know. We cannot claim that any of the historic homes we find in the Park date from 1086, but a very few – such as Duncton Manor Farm **(3)** – were built less than two hundred years later, many are on sites named in that survey, and much of that earlier history influenced where later houses were built and how settlements developed.

Although the record suggests there was still much unfinished business in 1086, the reorganisation had been carried out with more urgency in Sussex than anywhere else, as it was in the frontline for possible invasion. The county was divided into six north/south tracts of land or rapes, each based on a river, a port and a castle,

The Manor

The estate or *manor* was one of the earliest administrative units in England, even older than the parish. It was a word used to describe groups of land-holdings that varied widely both in size and structure, and initially the number of *hides* allocated (each roughly 120 acres) was a measure of its ability to pay tax. The land of a manor did not all have to be in the same place, but often included distant pieces of woodland or pasture, or even property within towns. *Demesne* land was the lord's 'home farm' as distinct from the lands of the villeins and sub-tenancies, and was generally exempt from tax. As part of the conditions of their tenancies, the tenants of the manor were expected to provide the labour to work the demesne, which could also employ tied servants.

Manorial *services* were onerous and related to the *tenement*, or the *virgate*, and the tenant had to carry them out. A *virgate* could vary from 15 to 80 acres, depending on the quality of the land, but in the south-east it generally approximated to 30. The tenant was responsible for seeing that any work for the lord was performed, using as many members of the family as he could muster, or by paying a sum of money in lieu. *Services* could include not only providing labour on the lord's demesne, but also carrying firewood and produce to other estates owned by the lord, driving animals to and from pastures and working ferries, and this was over and above what the tenant needed to do to run his or her own holding. By the 13th century most services were commuted to money payments. The *cottar* with *toft* and *croft* (cottage and enclosure) might hold about 5 acres, and then hire himself out as a wage-earner, or engage in some specific trade or occupation, such as shepherd or blacksmith.

The business of the manor was originally conducted at three-weekly *courts*, which tenants were obliged to attend or pay a fine. These courts were held in a manor house, and presided over by the lord or his *steward*. The *custom* or practice of a manor was written down from time to time, often when ownership changed, and could vary from place to place, but *fines* or fees could be levied on almost every event in a tenant's life. Particularly hard was the *heriot* or death duty when the best (or only) animal could be taken.

Customary tenancies became known as *copyhold*, because a tenant's title was a copy of an entry in the court book of the manor. Some manor courts continued to meet at longer and longer intervals until the 20th century; copyhold tenure was not finally abolished until 1924. *Freeholds* were on the whole held by money rent, had few practical obligations, and could be sold, leased or bequeathed without reference to manorial custom. Only in the late 19th and 20th centuries, when land or tenancies were legally *enfranchised*, did they become freehold in the modern sense. Discovering which manor a property belonged to can help towards unpicking the reasons behind its existence: why it was built where it is, when and by whom; when occupants changed and incomers could have made alterations.

3. Duncton Manor Farm: an early house with aisles. Dendro-dating has shown that the roof was largely re-framed in the 1360s, and details within the building suggest that by then it was already at least 80 years old, making it the oldest house identified in the South Downs National Park. The stone facing and casing is later.

making use of existing land divisions. There have been all kinds of theories about what a rape meant, including an area of land measured with ropes, but here it is enough to say that it is a unique term and dates from before the Normans arrived. A recent writer has described the rapes as 'largely mysterious'. These blocks of land were granted to powerful (and at first loyal) followers of William, all of whom also held land elsewhere, some in neighbouring Hampshire, such as

Roger de Montgomery, earl of Shrewsbury and Arundel, William de Braose, lord of Bramber and William de Warenne, lord of Lewes and Earl of Surrey. Within the rapes were the hundreds – originally an Anglo-Saxon sub-division of a shire – and within the hundreds were the estates or **MANORS**. It is the abbreviated and formalized description of these 'manors', that make up the entries in the Domesday survey, which can be represented by dots on a map **(4)**. The survey was mainly

concerned with how much each manor was worth, measured in terms of arable, pasture and meadowland, woodland, mills and fisheries, and who were the principal tenants, liable to pay geld (land tax) and to serve the king, as well as whether that income could be increased. The names can be plotted roughly with dots on a county map, and many of the dots are the villages and towns we know today.

The eastern part of Hampshire that bordered onto Sussex was less structured – both in the way in which the manors were distributed and the more 'jigsaw-like' arrangement of its hundreds, which in several cases were divided into parts that were scattered within the shire. Nevertheless, a browse through any of the books on local place-names of towns, villages and even individual farms in Sussex will find that many of them have Anglo-Saxon origins.

A first glance at the Domesday map of Sussex seems to support the idea that there were few people living in the woodland to the north of the Downs (very few dots) but from other evidence – such as archaeology and documents – we know that this was not true. The names of places south of,

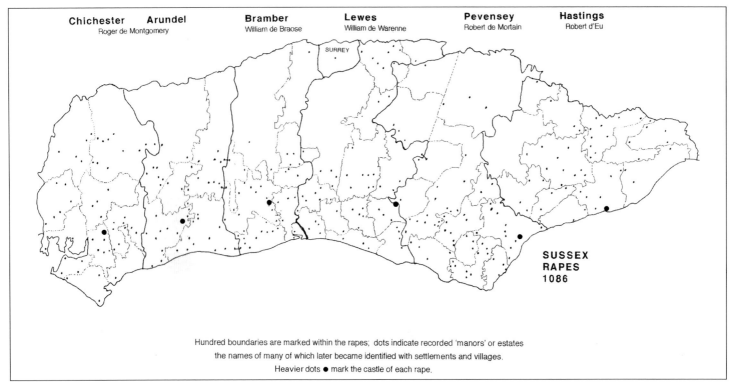

Chichester **Arundel**
Roger de Montgomery

Bramber
William de Braose

Lewes
William de Warenne

Pevensey
Robert de Mortain

Hastings
Robert d'Eu

SURREY

**SUSSEX
RAPES
1086**

Hundred boundaries are marked within the rapes; dots indicate recorded 'manors' or estates
the names of many of which later became identified with settlements and villages.
Heavier dots ● mark the castle of each rape.

4. This map is based on the 'Domesday' survey of 1086; each dot represents a manor, and many of the names are those of villages and towns we know today. The name of each rape, the same as the name of its dominant castle, is given in bold above the map.

or close to, the Downs, specially near the coast, suggest that these were the oldest settlements, which had a bearing on what happened to the north. This is especially true of many of the names ending in '-ing' – once the Anglo-Saxon '-ingas' – meaning 'the people of' or 'the tribe of': so we find Goring, Poling, Ditchling, Tarring and Washington.

The lives of most of the population revolved around agriculture, and an important part of early agriculture was the practice of transhumance. This meant driving animals (especially pigs) into woodland that might be 10 or more miles away, to take advantage of seasonal pastures and other resources, such as timber and stone for

A cottage at Selborne with coursed stone blocks, 'galleting' in the mortar joints and brick trim beneath thatch.
It is possible that the datestone (T S E 1793) relates to the masonry facing rather than the original build.
The raised centre initial usually represents the surname.

Stone Quarrying

Outcrops of stone were readily available in various localities, such as near Midhurst, Petworth, Pulborough and Horsham, and could be exploited by the estates who owned the quarries. The Domesday survey mentions quarries at Iping, Stedham and Grittenham (near Tillington) and another belonging to Bignor for millstones. Another quarry at Chithurst was given for the building of Durford Abbey, near Rogate, between 1160 and 1190. The better the final finish given to stone, the more labour was needed and the more likely that the product was for use on buildings of high status. Randomly-coursed stone rubble was employed for underpinning sills, and for repair and maintenance on buildings lower down the social scale. From the 1700s onwards worked stone blocks were being used to completely encase older timber houses, as well as for building from scratch.

building, underwood fuel, iron ore, honey, fruit, nuts and small prey animals. After centuries of these traditional movements, the seasonal herdsmen gradually became pioneering settlers and the 'home farms' regarded areas in the woods as belonging to them. Some of these small footholds may be represented by places like Glatting or Bargham, listed as manors in 1086, but where there are now just single farms, and by one of the four entries for Goring, which is actually described as an outlier. When the Domesday survey was carried out, the assets of those 'outliers' in the Weald were included within the record of the parent settlement, hidden as it were, and usually only traceable as *'pigs' worth of woodland'*. But without a doubt there were people up there in the woods, making clearings, wresting a living from the heavy clay of the Weald, digging stone, and most importantly, helping to harvest the timber and wood for building and fuel down south. These linkages between the scattered elements of a manor that provided different resources must also be reflected in the divided hundreds of Hampshire. The tenants of the outliers had to deliver produce and pay rents to their landlords in the older coastal settlements and sometimes place-names in conjunction with later surviving records, can give clues. The links between Bognor and the various Bignors further north, Poling with Palling-ham and Palling-hurst, Climping and Clemsfold, Goring with Goringlee are among the most obvious examples.

A good example of these sometimes surprising connections is a small, unassuming farmhouse close to the parish boundary between Petworth and Kirdford. **Buckfold** is understood to mean an animal enclosure (*fold*) within beech (*boc*) trees, and from records in the 1200s we know there were nine tenants there farming over 200 acres – and these are the records of the manor of **Bosham**. This large and important manor, which can be traced back to the 700s, was held before 1066 by King Harold's father, Earl Godwin, and was in King William's hands in 1086; among its many assets listed then was *6 pigs' worth*

5. This house at Buckfold illustrates several transitional (ie dated to the 1500s) features: proportions of the roof to the walling, brick bond using 'burnt' headers, hipped ends to the roof, corbelled and multi-flue chimney, small added lean-to at the right. The 'baffle-entry' and stair are both on this side of the stack, and raised brick letters at the rear date the brickwork to 1829–59.

responsible for many aspects of people's lives, including the upkeep of roads and poor relief. Parishes north of the Downs were often larger than those to the south, because (almost) invariably they had been established later and imposed upon a pattern of outliers that already existed. To the north of the Downs it is unusual to find that the boundaries of parish and manor are the same, as is often the case further south. This shows up particularly in parishes such as Lurgashall, Kirdford and Wisborough Green, which were made up of land and property divided among many manors to the south. Greatham near Parham is a rare exception, as an example of a manor house with its church and land all contained within its parish boundary.

of woodland. This must have been part of the earliest Buckfold farm **(5)**.

After the estate or manor, the next most important unit of administration was the **PARISH**, for this was a time when the Church and its beliefs were woven tightly into the fabric of everyday life. By about 1200, the parish system that was to last for the next 600 years or so was more or less in place, and everyone had to pay *landscot* (the parish rate) and burial fees. Eventually the parish was to become very much like the local council of the 20th century,

Summary

The lie of the land, the growth and decline of local economies and centuries of social and political activity have influenced where houses were built and the shapes of settlements. Transhumance and co-operative agriculture, groupings such as hundreds and rapes geared to national taxation and maintaining law and order, the organization of manor and parish,

The Parish

Early Christian administration was based on a pattern whereby the population was served by groups of 'missionary' priests living together at certain strategic points, with churches provided by the king or important laymen. These can sometimes be identified by historical or surviving designations as a 'minster', or from early references to their 'subsidiary chapels', which later became parish churches in their own right, with their own churchyard and charging burial fees. It has been said that *the early minster parishes were based directly on the pattern of royal administration, and the great mass of rural churches were a product of developing local lordship*'.

From the early history of the Christian church in England, the patron of a parish church had been entitled to 'tithe' the parishioners for income to maintain the fabric of the building, and to pay for services and the duties of a priest. This meant he could claim a tenth of all local produce, which was divided into the 'great tithes' (corn and hay) and the 'small' or lesser tithes (livestock, wool and non-cereal crops). Initially all these payments were in kind, but by the 1600s there was already some cash substitution.

Before the Reformation, the 'advowson' of a church (the right to take any income and to appoint a priest) could be held by the 'rector', who might be a landowner, such as the king, a bishop or the lord of a manor, and could be granted by him to an individual, not necessarily in holy orders, or an institution, such as a college or monastery. When institutions 'appropriated' parishes, they kept the great tithes as 'rector', and were expected to use the small tithes to pay a 'vicar' to serve in their place. After the Dissolution of the Monasteries many such rights were purchased from the Crown by lay people, and in these cases the separation between rector and vicar (and their incomes) could continue.

all these have to be brought together to appreciate fully what we find today. Above all, we have to remember that the houses we see now do not look as they did when they were first built, and the views we see today are rarely what the resident of times past saw when he or she looked out of the front door.

To appreciate local buildings more fully, we must not only look at how they were constructed and from what materials, but also at the shapes of settlements, how houses of different ages are distributed, and how they might relate to what was the earliest public building – the parish church.

Building Structure

If you want to see historic homes in the south-east more or less as they were first built, there are two places within the South Downs National Park you can visit – Butser Ancient Farm in the Queen Elizabeth Country Park at Chalton (Hants) and the Weald and Downland Open Air Museum at Singleton (W Sussex) – but bear in mind that these concentrate on different time spans. The buildings at each place are like templates and cannot hope to provide all the possible variations, but you can get some idea of how they looked when they were first built, and the numerous threads that have been spun together to produce what may be called the *'vernacular architecture'* of the South Downs. You need to start with the bones (ie the main structural timbers) – or what you can guess of them – and then go on to the flesh and skin (ie the material covering the façades), which has probably been adapted, modified, changed and replaced over the centuries. Many houses become like people who are heavily disguised. The older a house, the more changes are likely to have been made, and the further it will be from its original form.

Most of the surviving early buildings to be found in the South Downs National Park were constructed from prefabricated frames of oak timbers, the spaces filled

Timber

Wood was the all-purpose medieval material, much like plastics for us today. For example, *timber* was used for building – scaffolds, houses, bridges, mills, siege machines, ships – *underwood* for every imaginable tool, for vehicles, furniture, wattle panels, for household and industrial fuel or charcoal, and side products like oak bark for tanning and acorns for grazing pigs. Such an important material could not be left to chance and woodland was being managed for centuries before the Norman Conquest. Regular coppicing of hazel, hawthorn and willow produced underwood in rotation, oaks were encouraged to grow to straight standards for timber, separately or scattered among the coppices. Whatever their walling, all houses have timber roofs and floors. The 'average' fully framed house, fashioned from timbers up to 20ft long, needed between 2-300 standards, while shaped timber for particular uses, such as curved bracing, was usually found in hedgerows.

In about 1280 the tenants at Amberley were expected to build a barn at their own cost although their landlord (the Bishop of Chichester) was to find a master carpenter. In 1305 all the tenants on another manor were directed to help cart timbers for repairing new houses or maintaining old ones, and in 1357 the timber of a house was sold for 16s 8d, when £1 was roughly equivalent to £350. In 1385 an agreement between tenants and their landlord in Lurgashall stated that *'they [were] to keep up the hall chambers and barn against wind and rain receiving needful timber from the said William Howyk by decision of three men; in default of supply of timber the said John Ster and Alice [were] not to be accountable for damage.'*

6. Typical of the transitional (ie dated to the 1500s) houses of Amberley; the right-hand bay was added to a house that had an end smoke bay. This house has been given the traditional lime-wash treatment.

in with woven wattles daubed with mud, and the whole lot regularly covered with lime-wash, partly as a preservative, partly as a fire-retardant. The black-and-white appearance of many houses is the result of misplaced Victorian enthusiasm, trying to copy a Midland tradition. In the south-east, as the overall lime-wash treatment weathered, it resulted in the oak developing a silvery colouring, which is more authentic. You can find three buildings that have been treated like this in recent years: one at the top of the High Street in Lewes, Frylands in

the parish of Coldwaltham and Ivy Cottage in Amberley **(6)**.

The important people in this kind of house-building were the carpenters and joiners. While most modern buildings are constructed from blocks and held together by gravity, timber-framed buildings are held together by their pegged joints, and in theory could be picked up, turned around and put down in one piece, although the infill would probably drop out. They could also be dismantled, moved and re-erected on different sites, and were so, long before building museums were established! While there are a few examples of early *aisled* buildings which were rather specialised constructions, such as Duncton Manor Farm, dating from the end of the 1200s or early 1300s and later encased in stone, two of the predominant forms can be seen in the Park – cruck houses and box framing – of which the latter is the more usual.

Cruck framed houses are based on a series of pairs of long curved timbers fastened together at the apex in A-frames, and linked by lengthways **purlins**, lodged on the backs of the **crucks**. The linkage at the apex can vary and provide clues to age and sequences of construction **(7)**.

7. This grainy archive picture shows a good example of a cruck-framed building in Herefordshire, contrasted with the jettied box-framing to the rear.

Walling and roofing is then framed against the outside of the crucks and purlins, and often the only external clue is a pair of curved timbers visible at one end of the building. The A-frames did tend to cramp the head-room of first-floor rooms in later adaptations. This style of construction is fairly widely spread throughout England, and is found as far as eastern Hampshire; there are obvious examples to be seen in Farringdon and Chewton, and some rather more hidden examples in Hambledon and Dogmersfield, which has been said to be the most easterly example. Studies have concluded that Hampshire's crucks were of better quality than in many other areas,

This building in Ditchling is the result of centuries of adaptation and change, amalgamating at least two early buildings. Its side-purlin roof construction can be seen on the right-hand gable.

8 This Ditchling crown-post is braced-up, suggesting it was over a two-bay hall; the sooting from the smoke of the open fire is evident, with a certain amount on the plastered partition behind.

9 A down-braced crown-post in a Ditchling house that was almost certainly on a closed (filled-in) truss; the bottom of a rising brace from the crown-post to collar purlin can just be seen at the top.

10 Another Ditchling crown-post that sat over a two-bay open hall; one up-brace has been replaced, but traces of sooting are still evident.

and were by no means used for humble buildings. For reasons which are not fully understood, houses with crucks have not been found further into the south-east, in Sussex and Kent, although an adapted form, described as base-crucks, was used for some early buildings with aisles.

Box framed houses are based on vertical frames in a series of units or bays, like open-work boxes joined together with horizontal timbers, then roofed and the spaces infilled, and this was the norm throughout south-eastern England. The size of these houses is described by the number of **bays** – a bay being the distance between two pairs of **principal posts.** Principal posts extend from ground **sill** to **eaves-plates** and are linked together at the top by a horizontal timber called a **tie,** and all the joints of the frame were fastened together with oak pegs.

Houses of this type in this area were generally constructed with a **crown-post** roof, hipped at each end. A crown-post stands upon the middle of each tie that links a pair of principal posts. A timber running the length of the house in the middle of the roof space – **a purlin** – is supported on these crown-posts. Each pair of rafters is pegged at the apex and linked by a **collar**, which rests across the purlin. The collars are generally **halved** with a **dove-tail** against the rafters; less often they are tenoned into mortices **(8, 9 & 10)**.

Roofs – thatch, tiles and stone

Before 1800, most of the population of the South Downs was employed in agriculture in one way or another. Straw was a valued by-product for all manner of uses, and it is likely that until the 1550s, most buildings were originally thatched, and villages like Amberley and Houghton illustrate what was the norm. Before the development of modern strains of cereals, the stems were a lot longer – so much so, that modern thatchers have often turned to growing their own long-straw materials. When houses needed re-thatching it was usually only the upper layers that were replaced, and, to date, one house has been found with a smoke-blackened bottom layer of thatch, from the time when its only heating was an open hearth in the hall; there may be more out there to discover.

Clay tiles were not in general use until the 1400s, and then principally on the houses of the well-to-do; as commercial production was stepped up from the 1550s, alongside brick, so they became cheaper and more widespread. Split sandstone for roofing (mainly quarried around Horsham) was a valued alternative to thatch and tile, expensive enough to be used much further afield and carefully reclaimed wherever possible. In the 1600s, stone 'healers', the specialist roofers, were paid three times the average wage. The weight of such roofs determined the angle of the roof slope: no more than 45 degrees. Both tiles and stone slates were hung from roof battens with oak pegs, and the latter were laid with the smaller sizes near the top, a considerable overlap and lime mortar 'bedding'.

Two *bay* posts, a *tie* that linked them at the top, a *sill* that linked them at the bottom and another horizontal *tie* in the middle made up a **truss.** These trusses could be *closed*, that is filled in with shorter timbers and wattle-and-daub panels, or left *open*, without a middle tie, as over a two-bay hall or the first floor room at a floored end. On an open truss the crown-post was usually braced up four ways, to collar-purlin and collar, and the tie is often cambered, although there are always exceptions to prove the rule. The bay posts of an open truss had curved braces up to the tie from about half-way down the posts, forming an arched shape over the hall. Crown-posts braced up four ways can also feature over the middle of two-bay floored cross-wings, although the up-bracing from the posts in these cases is usually in the form of two short brackets rather than long braces **(11)**.

The crown-post on a closed truss was usually braced down to the tie, and up to the collar-purlin, with the principal posts braced down from the **jowl** to the mid-tie. Principal posts were generally jowled or thicker at the top, in order to accommodate the complicated jointing of **eaves-plate, post** and **tie**. This thickening was achieved by using a quartered tree-trunk with the root end at the top, and is sometimes described as a **root-stock**. The

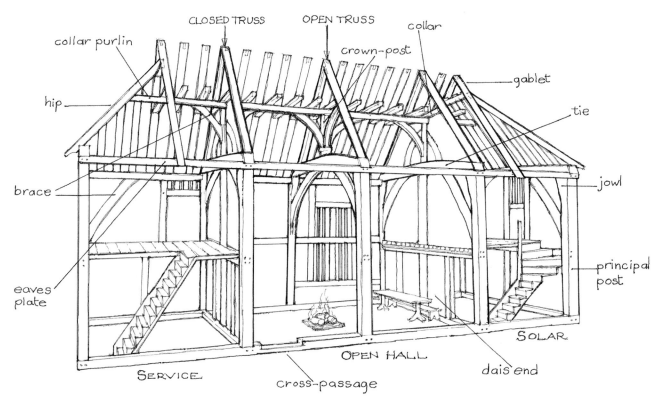

11 This illustrates an 'average' 4-bay house, with a 2-bay unfloored open hall at the centre.

profile of these jowls can help towards determining a date range.

Contrary to popular and enduring myth, timber-framed houses were not built from *'old ship's timbers'*, although a rare documented case of such a practice is Chesapeake Mill at Wickham, north of Southampton. There timbers from an eighteenth century prize ship, being broken up in the port in 1819, were salvaged for a new mill house. It is just possible that a few individual timbers were used as lintels for flint and brick cottages in coastal settlements, but the empty mortices and

PLEASE SHUT THE GATE

HONEYPOT COTTAGE

This appears at first to be a simple post-medieval end chimney house at Duncton, but evidence for changes can be seen on this elevation. The right-hand chimney has almost certainly been built into an earlier smoke-bay; herring-bone brickwork has replaced wattle-and-daub infill in the framework to the right and the original doorway was further to the right. The left-hand side has been faced up with stone rubble, and internal evidence suggests this was a later replacement or extension. A single-storey lean-to has been added along the rear elevation. This was almost certainly called Parkemans, first mentioned in a deed of 1598.

redundant peg-holes that have given rise to this belief are a reflection of the thrift of our ancestors, who recycled materials from older buildings. The visitor to the Mary Rose at Portsmouth will see that the shapes of a ship's timbers were very different, and would have become 'pickled' with sea-water. One reason behind the misunderstanding may have been the practice, in the late 1600s, of using *'ships' timber'* as a quality description, just as *'marine ply'* is used today. After all, the woodland of the Weald that had been managed since time immemorial supplied an abundance of building timber, and port records for Arundel in the 16th century included frames for houses and barns that were being exported – examples of early 'flatpack'!

*"Box-framed buildings were the direct opposite of cruck-framed buildings. Most of their timbers were short, 20ft being the maximum length, and scantlings of 6in square were usual. **Timber from intensively managed woodland** suited these dimensions well, and timbers of more than double the scantling were exceptional, even for posts and tie-beams."*

(From) *The Traditional Buildings of England* **by A Quiney (1990)**

Summary

Because the building survivals we see today are several hundreds of years old, they have been modified, adapted, repaired and maintained over that time, often introducing materials – weather-board, stone, brick, flint – that concealed the original forms and reflected what was available and how much it cost. None more so than structures that have survived from before 1500. The challenge is to distinguish between what was original and what has been part of the on-going maintenance and adaptation, such as weather-boarding and tile-hanging, brick infilling, under-building and encasing, clay tiles in place of thatch. Some of these adaptions have introduced different characteristics to buildings.

How Old Is It?

It is best to approach the changes that have happened to buildings with some kind of historical order in mind, although this will be rather artificial and has to be used in a flexible way.

- From the early part of the 1200s to soon after 1500, buildings were constructed that can be described broadly as '**medieval**', but fewer buildings survive from this earliest period, and those that do very probably belonged to the well-to-do in society.

- The century from 1500 to 1600 was a '**transitional**' period, when people were experimenting with adaptations of existing buildings and developing new forms that were then reflected in new builds.

- Greater numbers of buildings survive from 1600 onwards, the '**post-medieval**' period, partly because the houses being built from scratch had plans and proportions that are more familiar to us today and easier to adapt to modern living.

Medieval

During this time all but the houses of the very wealthy were built without chimneys, the only form of heating being an open hearth placed on the floor of a large room at its centre, which had no first floor – that is, it was open from ground to rafters – forming the *open hall*. This provided space for the smoke to drift up and filter out through the roof covering and the *gablets,* those triangular openings formed at the apex of the hipped roofs. Visitors to the Weald and Downland Museum at

Manor House

This is a term that can be used very loosely and be misleading. Domesday 'manors' did have a principal dwelling where the regular 'courts' were held, and where the lord of the manor or his representative lived. This was often close to a church; early survivals are almost unknown, but their replacements over time were usually on or near the same site. After 1086 some manors evolved from outliers or 'knights' fees', that is land held in return for military service, and a few of these established small churches or chapels for their tenants. Some of these little churches went on to become parish churches, such as Chithurst and Greatham, others only survive as a single reference or a field name, such as at River (whose early manorial name was Treve) near Tillington, or Rackham, near Amberley. So a 'manor house' or 'manor farm' may be a genuine successor to the early estate 'headquarters', particularly when the historical structure is supported by written sources, but in other cases the term may just describe an impressive building that has no real manorial significance.

Singleton will see how this smoke sooted the timbers; sooted timbers in the roof of a house that is still being lived in are often the only tell-tale sign that it once had an open hall. During that early period the word 'hall' often simply meant 'house', and it has come down to us meaning no more than the space behind the front door. There could be **bays** partitioned off from either or both ends of the hall, and if they were floored, each needed its own stair or ladder. The only windows were unglazed openings divided with upright wooden mullions that could be shuttered. The most important were those letting light into the hall, and smaller ones were tucked under the eaves at the floored ends.

The occupants of the very earliest of these open hall houses may have used the open hearth for cooking, but more recently the evidence has been found for 'detached kitchens' – constructions set apart from the house for food preparation and cooking. These sometimes become 'attached' at a later period, or were even converted into another house, and their significance was lost. Incidentally, although fire must have been a hazard with such houses and the evidence for such accidents has been found, there are also contemporary

records of fines being imposed for allowing houses to become ruinous. This neglect could have been the consequence of famine or plague affecting population numbers and discouraging people from taking up tenancies, or because a wealthy tenant had amalgamated several holdings, and the houses were surplus to his requirements.

These, then, were the *open hall* houses that had developed from a simple, single room plan, and in this region those with box-frames generally had a **crown-post** roof,

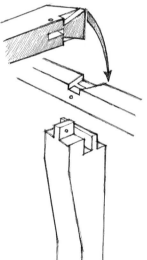

constructed with rafters joined together in pairs with **collars** which rested across a central **collar purlin** supported by **crown-posts** rising from the **ties** that linked the **bay posts.** Words used to describe the ways in which the different spaces in these houses were used have been borrowed from much grander buildings, like Penshurst Place; thus *solar, parlour* and *services* for the floored bays at each end of the hall, *low end* and *high* or *dais* end for the different parts of the hall, *cross-passage* and *screens* for the way between opposing doorways at the *low end* of the hall, which were, indeed, sometimes half-screened from the hall.

The wall framing of these houses was typically in large panels, with long curved diagonal braces, and the tops of the bay posts swelled into **jowls,** the better to take the jointing that was necessary at those important structural points where **eaves plate, tie rafter and post** all meet **(12)**. The

12 The 'teazel' joint is perhaps the most important in a box-framed building, linking bay post, tie, eaves-plate and rafter.

13 Looking across the open hearth towards the table at the dais or high end of the hall. The painted cloths to provide status were a cheaper alternative to panelling or woven tapestries. From the Weald and Downland Open Air Museum.

jowls at the top of bay posts were the result of quartering a single tree trunk and using the timber lengths upside down, the better to resist rot; hence an alternative name for *jowls* is *rootstocks*. The shape of these jowls can be a guide to the age of the building. From the second half of the 1400s *close-studding* was introduced, where a number of vertical timbers were set close together, particularly on the most visible sides of the house. This was not structurally necessary but it cost more and so was intended to impress!

Although open-hall houses were commonly rectangular in plan and single-pile – that is, one room wide – there could be variations in the ways in which the spaces or bays were arranged, as well as the distance between bay posts. The hall could have more than one bay; there could be floored bays at one or both ends of the hall; instead of floored end bays there could be cross-wings of one or more bays set at right angles. These variations resulted in different constructional details that can provide clues to the original form.

The open hall house reflected a society that had long revolved around communal living with little privacy, when most people were employed in agriculture, governed by the seasons and the weather. Medieval agriculture needed a great deal of co-operation within the community, to manage fairly its open fields, common grazing areas and shared meadows. It was also a youthful society – the average life-expectancy was about 35 to 40 – and death was a very familiar fact of life, so people were expected to become responsible adults much earlier than today, and aged more rapidly.

14 The 'garderobe' or upstairs en-suite 'loo' at the Weald and Downland Open Air Museum

There were opportunities within the houses of the well-to-do for the most important members to 'show off' in a limited way. Elements of the timber-framing could be shaped; the horizontal mid-tie at **the 'high' end of the hall (13)**, where the house-owner would set up his table at mealtimes, could be moulded along its length and the wall-space below panelled or hidden behind fabric hangings or paintings. Separate ground and first-floor rooms beyond that 'high' end became spaces where the owner could withdraw and do business, or sleep in more privacy with curtained beds. Sometimes he even enjoyed 'en suite' facilities at first floor, in the form of a **garderobe (14)**, such as that at Bayleaf in the Weald and Downland Open Air Museum.

The Wealden – a particular type

In estate agents' jargon, 'wealden' is used to describe almost any timber-framed house sited within the Weald of Kent, Sussex or Hampshire. For those who look at buildings, the term refers only to a particular type of building, best characterized by the house at the Weald and Downland Open Air Museum called Bayleaf. In its original form the Wealden house is easily recognised. Like the average open-hall house, it has a central portion that is without a first floor, which is flanked by floored ends. Generally it is roofed with hips at each end, but what creates its distinctive appearance is that the upper level of the floored ends are **jettied** forward – that is, they overhang the ground floor. Internally, the joists had to be arranged differently; instead of being

15 A house at Coldwaltham, with framework advertising its medieval origins, but later infilled with flint and underbuilt with brick.

16 This house in Byworth is clearly medieval, with a later chimney built in. Not quite so clear is that it is a Wealden, later converted to a continuous jetty.

18 This house at Filching is clearly a Wealden, with its recessed hall flanked by jetties, although one floored end has been modified or rebuilt. It has the storey-height close-studding much loved by those who wished to make a public statement.

17 The George at Alfriston, whose close-studding indicates a date of c.1480. Curved braces below the inn-sign suggest it may be a Wealden.

19 The Red Lion, Chalton: a good way to see a Wealden still in use, while enjoying a pub lunch!

20 Another house in Byworth with a continuous jetty that may be the conversion of a Wealden.

aligned longitudinally, which was the norm, they had to be aligned laterally, from a central girder. As the building had a single roof, the span of eaves plate in front of the central hall between the jettied ends needed extra brackets as supports, and a secondary eaves plate was introduced, giving the hall the appearance of being recessed, or set back.

This style clearly appealed to the aesthetic eye over a long period, for it persisted for nearly 200 years, becoming adapted for different sites and needs. Many remaining examples are extremely elaborate, with the jetties extending round the ends of the floored bays, needing the diagonal ceiling girder called a **dragon beam** to support the joists, some with the hall recessed on both long elevations and with all manner of decorative wall-framing. The plan was varied, just as with other houses, so that the hall could have one or two bays, and in some town situations the type was adapted to be built in 'terraces'.

When chimneys and first floors were introduced into the halls of Wealdens, the flanking jetties were often underbuilt, and the recessed wall of the hall brought forward to stand flush, so that the characteristic appearance can be almost completely disguised. Often the only remaining external clue may be the braces to the outer eaves plate, and internally, the arrangement of the joists in the floored ends. Fortunately a number of these buildings are still in use as public houses and restaurants – The Pilgrims Rest at Battle, The Swan at Fittleworth, The Red Lion at Chalton – so making them accessible.

Other Wealdens open to the public are **Ann of Cleves House in Lewes (owned by the Sussex Archaeological Society)**, and the first property bought by the National Trust – **The Clergy House at Alfriston** (see case study) – where decorative details suggest it was built in the early 1400s, possibly by the canons of Michelham Priory. Alfriston village contains a wealth of framed buildings, although not all are as apparent as The George and The Star Inns, which are also open to the public. The earliest example of a Wealden house known so far dates from 1340 (35, High Street, Winchester), and examples have been found in Coventry and as far north as York **(15, 16, 17, 18, 19, 20)**.

Transitional houses

One of the chief drivers for change to houses was the growing desire to contain the smoke from their open hearths. At first smoke was controlled and confined in existing houses by installing wattle-and-daubed framed partitions at first floor, creating hoods or narrow smoke-bays above the hearth, which could be moved from its central position towards the 'low' end. Later the open ground-floor hearths were contained within storey-height surrounds of stone and brick, and topped off with timber-framed funnels, all set within the cross-passage between the doorways at the low end. Surprisingly at least two examples have been found (in Hurstpierpoint and Billingshurst) of houses with framed smoke control still in place, although now with aluminium liners! In general, these could survive until there was the imagination and/or money to replace them with complete masonry chimney stacks – and hopefully before the house burnt down! A recent 'find' of a documentary reference that dates from 1556 tells of a lease being forfeit 'by the fall of the top of a chimney built of earth and chalk'. Innovations such as brick chimneys were clearly desirable and very much a status symbol, and early chimney stacks were often very prominent and frequently built with elaborate corbelled tops – over-sailing brick courses. The

Flint

Flint has been used since Roman times, particularly for foundations or rubble infill, but little survives from that period. In Saxon and medieval times coursed or randomly laid quarried and field flints were used with lots of lime mortar and in conjunction with dressed stone, particularly for churches. More decorative work with roughly broken and shaped flints alternating with stonework was introduced from the mid 1300s, as at Marlipins in Shoreham, and later still flints were also used like brick, to replace wattle-and-daub infill panels, but there are few comparable examples to the fine knapped flint and flush-work to be found in East Anglia.

Poor people were put to work gathering flints from the chalky fields, and flints were then used as a substitute for more costly stone, for replacing infill, refacing and under-building older timber houses,. At the time this must have been seen as long-lasting improvement, but the tension between the flexibility of timber framework and the rigidity of masonry could produce different problems, as water could penetrate cracks and accelerate rotting.

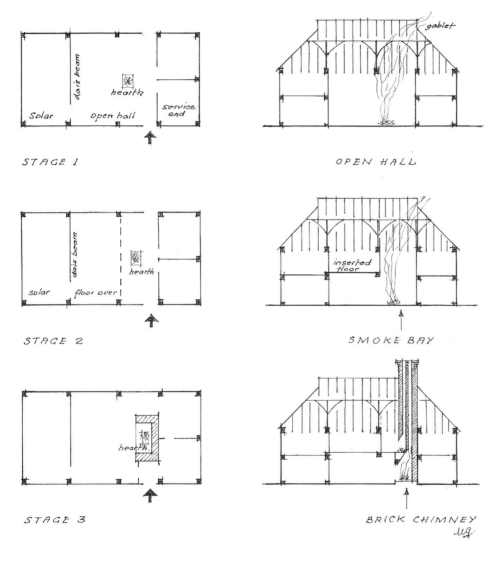

STAGE 1

STAGE 2

STAGE 3

Solar   dais beam   hearth   Open hall   service end

solar   dais beam   floor over   hearth

hearth

OPEN HALL

SMOKE BAY

BRICK CHIMNEY

gablet

inserted floor

relative position of a chimney stack, the number and arrangement of its flues/chimney pots and its quality can all be guides towards the date of its construction **(21)**.

Although the move towards hearths with masonry surrounds and chimney stacks was welcomed, people did seem to have some reservations, for this was a time when the division between the real and the spirit world was still blurred. At one time very little notice was taken of what appeared to be rather random markings on timbers, especially the timber bressumers over fireplaces **(22)**, but more attention has been paid over recent decades. These are now described as *apotropaic* or ritual markings, which were made deliberately to protect against evil spirits who might find their way into a house through the 'new entrance' – the chimney. The marks are often variations on a daisy wheel, or

21 These plans and sections are a simple introduction to the way in which timber-framed buildings developed from the medieval open-hall to the fully-floored house with a multi-flue chimney stack.

22 The fire is ultimately confined within an enclosed hearth with a chimney stack to funnel the smoke.

Weald and Downland Open Air Museum.

Windows

Early windows generally had diamond-shaped vertical wooden mullions, and the style persisted until the mid 1600s. They were generally unglazed, with shutters that could slide horizontally or be hinged. Some evidence has been found of using small sheets of worked horn and scraped animal skins for smaller windows, to give a degree of light without letting in the weather. Even when glazing became more widely available, this was sometimes confined just to the windows that 'showed'. Some of the earliest sash windows were introduced towards the end of the 1600s, generally on larger houses, and were seen as a great improvement on wrought iron and leaded casements. They tended to have heavy glazing bars and only the lower sash operated. Window taxes were imposed from 1696 onwards, and were not finally repealed until 1851, but they were not the reason for all blocked windows. Some were the result of changes to internal spaces, others were planned to produce a symmetrical frontage, and were sometimes painted to look like windows.

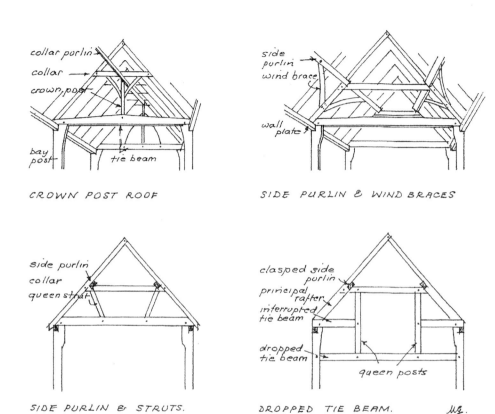

collar purlin
collar
crown post
bay post
tie beam

CROWN POST ROOF

side purlin
wind brace
wall plate

SIDE PURLIN & WIND BRACES

side purlin
collar
queen strut

SIDE PURLIN & STRUTS.

clasped side purlin
principal rafter
interrupted tie beam
dropped tie beam
queen posts

DROPPED TIE BEAM.   MG.

23 This shows variations in roof construction.

the initials VM for Virgin Mary, and have also been found by other openings, such as doors and windows. Research into these markings is now being extended to studies of so-called 'taper burns', which may come

into the same category. Of course there are also personal initials and dates to be found, although these may not always be historically valid!

Other changes and improvements followed on as the results of the control of smoke. A first floor could be introduced into halls which no longer needed to be open; this usually meant that both sets of stairs to upper rooms at each end were no longer necessary, and flights could be removed or re-sited. With increased use of the extra levels of houses came changes in the placement of windows: for instance, the old double-height hall windows were halved by inserted first floors, and some were replaced with bay windows. As glass became more widely available the sizes and siting of windows changed, particularly on the front of a house, where display mattered.

Roof construction changed as people sought to make their attic space habitable. The old timber-heavy medieval construction, with its collars to every pair of rafters, braced crown-posts and a purlin down the centre, were replaced by side-purlins running along each side of the roof which only needed collared partitions at the bay divisions; half-hips and gables took over from hips. Fortunately for the student of buildings, who spends a great deal of time crawling through attic spaces, the roofs over early

24 The gables of this Winchester building (Chesil Rectory) illustrate the characteristic 'butterfly bracing' to side-purlins of medieval buildings in Hampshire.

houses that were adapted often survive completely or partially, even when the structure below has been changed and concealed. Patterns of wall framing also began to change, moving towards smaller, more regular square panels with shorter diagonal braces and less substantial timber, reflecting increasing demands on resources **(23)**.

For reasons that we cannot entirely explain, between Hampshire and Kent the change from crown-post roofs to those with side-purlins happened earlier in the west and moved slowly eastwards. In Hampshire the move away from crown-posts came in the 1400s, and a range of side-purlin styles can be found over houses that were still built with open halls. Although side-purlins have been found over open halls in Sussex, they tend to be later than the Hampshire examples, and more common towards the west. A study of houses in Harting parish found that of nine medieval buildings, only one had a crown-post – all the rest had Hampshire style 'butterfly' bracing with side-purlins, as can be seen on the gables of Chesil Rectory, Winchester **(24)**.

Old houses were adapted and the changes that were made were then incorporated into houses built towards the end of the transitional period. If the money was available, a more radical change could be made by completely replacing the open hall, particularly if its early proportions made it difficult to adapt, and even more so if there were cross-wings that could be retained with the replacement.

The end of this period saw people begin to put dates on the changes they had made, such as on the bressumers over new inglenook hearths, on additional wings or new doors and windows, and this practice gradually became more widespread. Oakhurst Cottage at Hambledon, owned by the National Trust, offers guided tours to see inside a low-status cottage.

Glass

Glass making began in Surrey in the 1200s, close to plentiful fuel supplies for firing the kilns and sandy soils for producing potash. It expanded in the late 1500s to parishes such as Kirdford, Northchapel and Wisborough Green, although it was very small scale and monopolised by a few secretive immigrant families. It was the increased demand for window glass during the Transitional period of house building that promoted the growth of a home-grown industry. At first only small panes could be produced, which influenced the shape and form of windows – hence 'leaded lights'. Men described as 'glass maker' and 'carrier' [quarrier] begin to appear in local parish registers from the last quarter of the 1500s, and some men with related skills diversified into it. In 1602 two Woolavington brickmakers delivered *'one load of hole broad glasse of the best to glasse windows'* to an Arundel draper. In 1671, the antiquarian John Aubrey wrote that *'Glass is becoming more common in England. I remember that before the civil wars, ordinary poor people had none. But now the poorest people on alms have it . . . Soon it will be all over the country'.*

25 The left-hand bay is an addition to a four-bay house in Tillington. Although half of the original building has been rendered, the window pattern is consistent, with a narrow chimney bay at each end. The position of the first-floor window heads and the vertical studs show this has a deep dropped-tie roof construction, creating a fully usable attic. It is underbuilt in stone and brick; there is evidence for a front door at each end, when it was in dual occupation.

Post-medieval

From 1600 onwards, the '**post-medieval**' period, the way houses were built and organised becomes closer to what we are familiar with, as the changes of the transitional period were built in from scratch. As society moved away from communal living towards wanting more privacy, and placing value on an individual personal space, partitions were introduced to form passages and doorways were adjusted, so that occupants no longer needed to move straight from room to room. Outside, clusters of brick chimney stacks, glazed windows, porches and storeys throughout announced to all that these were houses in the latest style, although some of the dates that can be spotted on chimney stacks are as late as the 1700s, and show just how long framed solutions could remain in use. Back-to-back hearths at ground and even first-floor levels acted like central heating. Front doors opening onto one side of the new chimney stacks (the *baffle* or *lobby entry*), and stairs winding up within the same space could 'free up' the living areas.

Brick & Bonds

After the Romans, building with bricks did not revive till the later Middle Ages – at first very locally, where there was access to suitable clay deposits and underwood for firing simple clamps and kilns. The 1530 will of Sir David Owen of Cowdray specified that a brick vault should be constructed *'where his body shall lie underground'*, there are numerous references to brickmakers of Woolavington from the second half of the 1500s, and men described as 'bricklayers' start appearing in parish registers about the same time. Demand grew with the search for materials for newly introduced chimneys and porches, for under-building and facing older timber houses, and for quoins and the surrounds to windows and doors in flint walling. Bricks were traditionally baked in stacks with fuel piled under and around them, which was then set on fire. The uneven colouring produced by bricks fired in these temporary kilns was exploited in diaper patterns in early brickwork, and in chequer patterns on humbler buildings, especially from the 1700s onwards.

BONDS describe how bricks are arranged when first laid. Early brick bonding tended to be irregular, but settled into 'English' bond – alternate courses of headers and stretchers – a style which lasted throughout the Tudor period and lingered into the second half of the 1600s. This eventually gave way to alternate headers and stretchers in the same course, or 'Flemish' bond. Some Georgian houses used header bond, but this was costly and so rare. Modern stretcher bond, described as bland and monotonous, is linked to the development of cavity walls. A tax was first imposed on bricks in 1784, resulting in large sizes and courses set on edge, and probably increased the use of weather-board facing on poorer cottages; it was finally repealed in 1850.

One of the most common changes in plan was the introduction of the single-storey 'lean-to' or 'outshot' along the rear elevation, and sometimes at the 'service' end, beneath long sloping 'cat-slide' roofs. These served a growing variety of household functions, and often appear in records named as bakehouse, brewhouse, milk house and wash-house. Outshots could be added to existing buildings, sometimes blocking earlier windows, or planned from the start, with usable lofts or space for a staircase.

As attics were brought into wider use, the desire for more head-room produced developments in roof construction such as the **dropped** or **interrupted tie,** where the attic floor was no longer at eaves level, but 'dropped' by anything up to three feet.

This is a case where roof construction can be guessed from outside; when the tops of first floor windows are well below the eaves level, it usually signifies a 'dropped-tie' **(25, 26, 27, 29)**.

It was during this period that the wattle-and-daub panels of frames began to be replaced with brick, stone and flints. This must have been seen as a wonderful

26 A house in Wisborough Green. The position of the first floor window heads shows that this has a dropped tie roof construction, and the 'wavy' ridge line is characteristic of the period before ridge boards were introduced. It is a framed building with a Horsham stone roof, faced with stone blocks; the courses of brickwork at first-floor (left) should alert researchers to the probability of some change in that area. The door is in the 'baffle-entry' position, onto the side of the chimney.

27 This attic in Ditchling shows a dropped tie roof construction with the attic floor level below eaves level; the interrupted tie has a metal strap to the vertical queen strut at the point that is most vulnerable to strain; the side-purlins are slightly staggered and butted into the principal rafter. Wind-braces from the principal rafter help to preserve rigidity.

option, being more durable and reducing the need for wearisome and regular replacement. Unfortunately it brought its own problems, for the tension between flexible framing and rigid masonry produced cracks which allowed in water and accelerated timber rot. The alternative of completely facing or casing the frame reduced this problem, which was costly and changed the character of the building, so that owners unwittingly neglected the maintenance needed for a timber house,

28 Two gabled fronts in Ditchling illustrate different kinds of infill. The right-hand building with its bracketed oriel window backs onto the churchyard, and contains medieval framing.

Iron

Before the advent of large-scale iron production in the Weald, in the late 1500s and into the 1600s, digging and processing iron ore was small-scale and very localised. Any ironwork that was needed in buildings, as for tools and other craftsmen like wheelwrights, was generally produced by blacksmiths, who were the 'aristocrats' of local communities. Although the most productive sites lie northeast of the South Downs National Park, the impact of the industry spread beyond the actual ironworks, which became transport hubs, and opportunities for a range of subsidiary employments developed such as forestry, as timber was coppiced and cut for fuel. The most visible remains of iron production are 'hammer ponds' in woodland, with several examples to the west of Midhurst, now tranquil survivals of what was once a landscape of heavy industry.

sometimes to their cost, as concealed timbers gently rotted away.

Increasing demands for building timber from a growing population and competition from industries like iron and glass-making meant lighter and shorter timbers for houses, and this influenced further changes. When inferior quality timber was used for walls and ceilings it was usually intended to be plastered over, and external walls would be weather-boarded or tile-hung, with the possible benefits of improved heat insulation, and protection against decay or weathering.

29 Near Burpham; the lefthand range of these flint cottages contains most of a medieval open hall house. The different roof lines and supporting historical information supplied the initial clues to this survival.

The Urban View

There are a number of towns within or just outside the Park, each with quite a distinct character. At either end are Winchester and Eastbourne, probably the most extreme contrast; the former an ancient Anglo-Saxon capital and cathedral city, the latter with traces of Roman and Domesday settlement in and around its Old Town, but chiefly developed by the Dukes of Devonshire from the 1850s. Petersfield, Midhurst, Petworth, Arundel, Steyning and Lewes are strung out in between: all had markets, and all were ancient boroughs, except for Petworth. The plans of all these towns were first and foremost influenced by the need for an open space for their markets, some of which are easier to spot than others; a wider than average street, sometimes colonised with an 'island' of buildings, is the best clue, as is a market house or hall, sometimes rebuilt more than once. Variations of plan can also reflect the impact of powerful landowners – the castles at Winchester, Midhurst (remnants at St Ann's Hill), Arundel and Lewes, the great houses at Midhurst (Cowdray) and Petworth – and their fortunes on the national stage. Both Petworth and Arundel

30 Looking along Church Street in Steyning, which with its high proportion of early buildings almost takes one back to the 1400s.

were significantly affected when their resident lords wished to enlarge their grounds, houses being demolished and streets re-aligned.

The differences between towns – and often whether they appear predominantly Georgian or Victorian – usually reflect the periods during which they were most successful and/or prosperous, and so

when their buildings were most likely to be altered or replaced. When burgesses travelled to trade and to attend the royal parliaments, they had opportunities both to hear about and see different styles of building **(28, 30)**. The fact that Steyning has a higher than average proportion of surviving framed buildings on designated 'burgage' plots could be because it became a 'pocket borough', providing

31 The Brotherhood Hall, Steyning, that was converted to a grammar school by 1614, has been dendro-dated to 1446–51.

MPs at the will of the Dukes of Norfolk. It eventually lost out commercially in competition with the port at Shoreham, and became something of an economic backwater. Steyning's Brotherhood Hall, dendro-dated to between 1446 and 1451, is a fine example of a merchants' guild headquarters, which is mentioned in 1548 when the chantries were dissolved under Henry VIII. It then became redundant, was sold off and by 1614 was converted for use as a grammar school **(31)**. Midhurst did not get its grammar school until 1672. At first a dozen poor boys met in a room in the market hall, which was already 120 years old.

Towns are rewarding for the 'house-detective' because their buildings can be viewed from different angles, and many are accessible to the public; just think of all those shops, tea-rooms, pubs and restaurants! As long as one shows some interest in the commercial offerings, there are opportunities to see examples of different kinds of wall and ceiling framing, as well as rare painted wall decoration in a Midhurst tea room, and an equally rare carving of a Green Man on a ceiling timber in Steyning Post Office. There is also a fine 17/18th century plastered ceiling in a restaurant on the High Street in Arundel.

At first sight there can be some comparison between buildings in urban and rural settings, for after all, the materials and techniques used were much the same. However, the restrictions of ancient plot boundaries laid out for administration and trading, and the demands of a market economy, such as the need for inns and increasingly specialised shop premises, resulted in different forms, plans and rates of development. The ubiquitous Wealden was developed in various ways: there are six in Steyning and three in Petworth **(32 & 33)**. 'Speciality' jettied buildings appeared, such as in Petersfield (The Donkey Cart); first the **continuous jetty**, medieval but without an open hall, often developed by ecclesiastical bodies keen to make a profit

32-33 Two of Steyning's Wealdens.

Borough, Burgage, Burgess

A town became a borough when it was granted the right to govern itself, by the Crown or its overlord, usually in return for an annual sum of money. It became a corporation, running weekly markets and yearly fairs, and policing local affairs through its own courts. All boroughs had markets, but not every market town was a borough.

The street plan of a borough was based on burgage plots or houses, whose owners, or burgesses, paid a ground rent and could buy and sell their property freely, and these were usually clustered around the market place. As frontages were valuable, burgage plots were often long and narrow, at right-angles to the street. The burgesses were the leading townsmen responsible for the borough's government, and from the mid-1200s could also choose representatives from among their number to attend the king's parliament, wherever it met. Initially these early MPs were genuinely local people, but with the developing importance of parliament in national government, powerful magnates would buy up burgages so that they could put in their own candidates, and many historic towns, such as Steyning, became 'pocket boroughs'. The corruption and manipulation of these voting systems did not begin to be addressed until the Reform Act of 1832 and in legislation that followed.

and usually providing commercial premises **(34)**; then the '**double-jetty**', where both first and attic storeys over-hung forward to make best use of a restricted ground plan. These could be impressive Transitional or Post-Medieval town houses for the well-to-do, such as on Lewes High Street. Hampshire can also boast an extraordinary development, which combined an open hall with a continuous jetty frontage, by forming a kind of internal gallery across the open hall; there are two in Wickham, others in Petersfield and Winchester, including the **Old Blue Boar,** and one has been identified over the Sussex border in Harting (Fowlers Buck) **(35-39)**.

34 A typical urban building in Steyning of continuous jetty with close-studding. Note the earlier window site and tile-hanging on the gable (see also 49).

35 A typical double-jettied town house in Lewes from the late 1500s or early 1600s, with three gables, its framing concealed with tile-hanging. The change in the pattern of tiling indicates either when the ownership of the building was divided, or that it was built in stages. Note the heavy glazing bars of the early sash windows, and first floor bay windows. The shop-fronts have underbuilt the jetty.

36 A double-jettied medieval town building in Lewes, renovated and lime-washed in the traditional way. Note the typical curved down-bracing to the left.

37 These town buildings in Midhurst illustrate the different faces of traditional buildings, from plaster render, through framing or tile-hanging above brick to simple coursed stone blocks with brick trim.

38 The market hall in Midhurst with the regular square framing, herring-bone brick infill and gabled roof characteristic of post-medieval buildings. This was the building used by the grammar school when first founded.

39 The Spread Eagle, Midhurst, which contains medieval timber-framing, can be seen beyond the old market hall.

Interiors

From the end of the Transitional period, you can imaginatively play a version of 'Through the Keyhole', peering (almost) into people's houses and getting an idea of how they lived. This is because those documents which listed personal possessions – 'goods and chattels' – and which were taken at the time of a person's death, survive in increasing numbers in local record offices from the beginning of the 1600s. These were the 'inventories' which were part of the paperwork needed to be granted probate. Here you can find the names that were given to different rooms, lists of furniture, household items, kitchen utensils, bedding and linen. If they were farmers, their stock and crops were included, or tools and goods if they were craftsmen or traders, and comparisons can be made between town and country, small farmers, yeomen and gentry.

1629 December Duncton
John Gounter, labourer
Appraisors: Geo Goble, Mich. Gittens, Rd & Jas Ayling

	£	s	d
Ite[m] in **the hall** one paire of pot hangers a paire of pothooks a fry ing pane a pair of gridirons a paire of tonges a spit a bill and an axe a spitter and a shovel two prongs a ioyned forme three chairs one cradle a grabbing beeke a spitter and a shovell		xvi *s*	
Ite in **the chamber** two bedsteddles two featherbeds three blanketts two Coverlets on fether bolster one flocke bolster three pillows	£v		
Ite fyve paire of sheets one sheete two tablecloths	£2	15 *s*	
Ite fyve Chestes		xvi *s*	16 *d*
Ite the peas **in the house**		xvi *s*	
Ite fyve pewter dishes five platters two pewter bowles 2 saltes 4 porrin gers one candlestick	£1		
Ite 2 kettles 2 brasse skilletts one brasse la dle a skimmer	£i	vi *s*	6 *d*
Ite three flitches of bacon one potte of honie	£i		
Ite iii tubbes iiii verkins 3 knives and a halfe bushell 3 trugges one bowle two bucketts		13 *s*	vi *d*
Ite two sythes and two sawes			ix *s*
Ite other lumber	£1		
Ite his waring apparel and the money in his purse	£2		
Ite twentie corde of wood	£iiii		
Ite fyfteene sheepe	£iiii		
Ite one Colte	£i	x *s*	
Ite one swine		viii *s*	
Ite the corne upon the ground	£2		
Ite in readie moneye in Walter Kings hands	£5		
Ite remaining in Walter Kings hands more		xvi *s*	
Ite for the lease	£1		
Ite three stales of bees		vi *s*	
Total	**£44**	**15**	**6**

Furnishings

To modern eyes early houses would have been very sparsely furnished. Probate inventories distinguish between *boarded* and *joined* furniture – indicating the quality of construction – and the frequent descriptions of tables as *'boards and trestles'* shows that these could be dismantled and stored aside, clearing the open halls for other activities once meals were over. Forms and stools which were also easily stored were for general seating, with occasional chairs that must have given status to the user. Bedsteads or 'steddles' with their corded bases covered with rush matting, sometimes curtained for extra insulation or privacy, were valued (and valuable) items and often appear in wills of the period; the 'bed' is what we would call the mattress and could vary in quality according to its filling. A low or truckle-bed could be stored underneath the principal bedstead, ready for a child, servant or visitor. The commonest pieces were various chests and boxes, which could double up as seating or be used for displays of treasured crockery or pewter. 'Carpets' were generally woven 'runners' placed along the tops of 'cup'-boards. 'Presses' begin to appear during the 1600s, and described the more elaborate side-boards with shelves. Household linen – sheets, towels, pillow *'coates'* or *'beeres'*, napkins – was another valuable item that was almost always separately listed and must have been stored in a dedicated chest. Like bedsteads linen often features in wills.

40 Chests and baskets were common forms of storage units.

Weald and Downland Open Air Museum.

These documents show how much beds and bedding were valued, so that leaving someone your second-best bed was not an insult! Apart from beds, furniture could be joined or boarded, reflecting its quality, and was generally restricted to trestle tables and forms, stools, a few chairs, boxes and chests. The range became more varied over the centuries, with the introduction of 'press cupboards', 'chests of drawers', round, oval and 'falling' (folding) tables, and different kinds of chairs – leather, wicker or rush and 'armed'. Household linen – sheets, pillowcases, tablecloths, towels – was

41 A chest called an 'ark', with a shaped lid that could be removed and used for mixing dough or salting items of food.

42 A bed with curtains for extra warmth and privacy, and high enough to store a simple truckle bed beneath.

Both images from the Weald and Downland Open Air Museum.

nearly always listed separately, and often described in detail, such as coarse, fine, tire or diaper. Some linen was embroidered with initials, showing how they were seen as heirlooms. Items like andirons, 'dogs', fire-pan, tongs and bellows can help to locate hearths; spits, pothooks, hangers and kitchen vessels tell us which were the 'cooking' hearths, and a gradual move from describing rooms as 'hall' or 'kitchen' reflects the change from open hall to fully floored houses.

By and large, 'chambers' were upstairs, and very often were related to the room they were above e.g. 'the chamber over the parlour.' With this in mind and a plan in hand, it can be possible to locate first-floor hearths, and even re-construct the lay-out of the house. From the middle of the 1600s onwards a greater variety of items begin to appear, including clocks, weapons like muskets and fowling pieces, glass and chinaware. This was of course a pre-decimal world, and the values were

in pounds, shillings and pence; that is, 12 pence to the shilling and 20 shillings to the pound. The example at the beginning of this chapter illustrates some of the characteristics of such documents; the erratic spelling and division of words (which depended on the size of the paper) obsolete words and odd mixture of Arabic and Roman numerals, and is best read aloud with a Sussex accent! **(40-45)**.

43-45 A chest could be simply boarded, decorated, or developed into a press. (From the Weald and Downland Open Air Museum at Singleton).

Beyond the 'vernacular'

The truly 'vernacular' period began to wane from the second quarter of the 1700s onwards, when at first better roads, then canals and finally railways meant that materials were more easily transported from place to place around the country, house-building became more commercialised with standardised plans and there was more general access to ideas from regional and national sources rather than just local traditions.

47 Behind the Georgian front range is the original timber-framed farmhouse (to the right). This was a favourite way of achieving visible 'modernisation' and impressing one's contemporaries, without losing living space.

46 An up-to-date Georgian stone farmhouse at Coldwaltham, with good original sash windows and a stone string course – but it is not all as it appears: walk around the side . . .

In the final decades of the 1600s, however, large houses were still being built at gentry level that made use of the opportunities for display offered by a decorative use of timber-framing, often only on the front elevation. As brick-making techniques improved and production became increasingly commercial, so bricks became more widely available, and timber-framed houses slid down the social scale.

Dendro-Dating

Dendro-chronology is the method of dating timbers by counting and comparing the growth rings of trees. If suitable samples can be taken it can be remarkably accurate in obtaining the date when the tree was felled, and we know that timber was used 'green' or within two years at most. A 'dendro' project has been carried out in Hampshire and admirably collated and assessed by Edward Roberts in his publication on Hampshire buildings, and some individual buildings have been successfully sampled in Sussex. Research programmes of this kind can complement and enlarge upon dating assessments arrived at by comparing a range of building features, although this latter process will never be completely redundant as there are still timbers that resist analysis or were re-used.

Old framed houses were disguised, sub-divided and used to house the labouring poor, while new cottages were smaller with masonry walling. The sub-divisions of houses often meant the introduction of extra doors, stairs and partitions, all designed to confuse the house detective!

The final knell sounded on centuries of traditional construction with the introduction of houses that were double-pile – two rooms thick — and the changes in roofing patterns that this made necessary. This could range from the M-roof over parallel ranges through variations on pyramidal solutions, and often involved internal guttering. However, there are examples to be seen of local interpretations of this development, such as Idehurst in Kirdford, Waltham Farm in Coldwaltham and the Manor of Dean in Tillington, where 'modern' masonry ranges have been built in front of an old house, or its remnants, which has been kept but down-graded to provide ancillary rooms **(46 & 47)**.

In the main, the only distinctive local buildings that continued to be built were probably the cottages built for their tenants by the great estates – Cowdray, Goodwood, Petworth and Arundel – in various combinations of brick, flint and stone, and often with identically coloured paintwork.

Documents

what there is and where to find it

Although this book is mainly concerned with introducing readers to the buildings they will find in the South Downs National Park, and their place in the landscape, mention has been made of other influences upon their development: landlords and occupants, changes in fashion and function, the need for repair and maintenance, the ups and downs of the local economy. Once you have got into the habit of looking at buildings with more understanding, you will probably realise there can be more to this than (literally) meets the eye. The single example of a probate inventory has already been used to show what can be gleaned from one such record, and there is much more.

Where can you go to find more information? The two main sources are your local library and county record office, and currently both are still free. (The record offices that cover the area of the Park are at Winchester, Chichester and Falmer). The first contains mainly published material, most notably volumes of the 'Buildings of England' series (by county), often just known as 'Pevsner' after the pioneer of the concept. Most libraries of any size will have a 'local studies' area, where you can find information about the general history of the area, much of it presented under 'parish' headings. 'Parish' can mean two things: the historical land unit, focussed on the parish church, or the more modern 'civil parish'. The boundaries are probably not identical, but they have one thing in common; both are (or were) concerned with local administration. In among 'local studies' you may also find the Sussex and Hampshire volumes of the Victoria County History, and the printed volumes produced by the county historical and archaeological societies. The latter vary from collections of essays and articles published annually for decades, to printed original documents, such as those produced by the Sussex Record Society – a great help to those who may be put off by a glimpse of historical handwriting and medieval Latin! Other information, such as directories, census returns and newspapers, may be available on microfilm or fiche.

The record office will also have some printed material, but the bulk of their collections are original documents held in their strong rooms, including all kinds of ecclesiastical records (both parish and diocese), manorial papers, collections from local solicitors' offices, those of great estates such as Goodwood, Petworth and Cowdray, historic sale particulars and the multitude of items that come under 'Add Mss' or 'AM' (Additional Manuscripts). This may seem daunting to begin with, but there will be staff at hand to help guide you through the process of first identifying the material you want to consult, and then putting in your request – 'ordering it up'.

Record office search rooms are also full of catalogues, both printed and in files. These are grouped under headings – subjects, places or collection – and include short summaries of the documents to which they are acting as a guide. Nowadays most record offices have embraced the process of putting these lists on-line, so that investigators can search at home in preparation for a visit. The document summaries can sometimes provide a good idea of the contents, but there is usually no substitute for seeing the original, although you will need to become familiar with a different terminology, such as messuage, tenement, lease and release, customary

Tithe Records

From the 8th century it was a legal obligation on Christians in England to give one-tenth of all produce to the church. Originally the great tithes of corn and hay and small or lesser tithes of livestock, wool and non-cereal crops went to the rector, who maintained the chancel and made provision for worship, but these rights could be granted as a gift to an individual or corporate body, or bought and sold. When the rector – who held the 'advowson' or right to present an incumbent – was a layman or institution, he expected to take the great tithes, while the lesser tithes were intended to pay the vicar who served in his place. After the Reformation, tithe-rights which had been owned by monastic houses were confiscated and sold to lay 'impropriators', and increasingly tithes or their collection were owned by laymen, or by absentee, pluralist clergy (those who were appointed to more than one parish). This created growing resentment and opposition among parishioners to payment of tithes.

From the seventeenth century onwards various local arrangements were negotiated for money payments in lieu of tithes, and Parliamentary enclosure acts between 1757 and 1835 offered further opportunities to reduce ill-feeling by allotting land in lieu of tithes. The Tithe Commutation Act of 1836 was intended as the final solution to the problem which had rumbled on for so long, by converting all tithes to rent charge payments based on the prevailing price of grain. As a result of this Act, most parishes were surveyed over the next ten years to produce large-scale maps with accompanying schedules, which included landowner, occupant, description of the property and land use. Every field, building, lane and feature was numbered, described and entered in the schedule, with landowner and occupant, and the names often enshrine historical details. Three copies were produced for each parish – for the parish clerk, for the diocesan bishop (both now usually kept at the local record office) and for the tithe office (now at The National Archive at Kew). About 79% of England and Wales is covered by these maps **(48)**.

and copyhold, uses and fines – but specialist dictionaries will be at hand.

From the 1800s onwards documents are generally legible, if not printed, but if you want to travel further back in time you will need to discover palaeography – the study of early handwriting. You can battle on using available guides and actual examples,

like wills and probate inventories, but many record offices will offer inexpensive one-off sessions or short courses.

The houses in the South Downs National Park that have been introduced in this book existed in a time when religious belief and the church were an inextricable part of everyone's life, and because the

parish was once the only body roughly equivalent to the local council, its records will include far more than just the original registers of baptisms, marriages and deaths. Most of these registers are fully transcribed and indexed, and can often include little extra gems of information, such as a person's trade or position. There can also be information about the upkeep

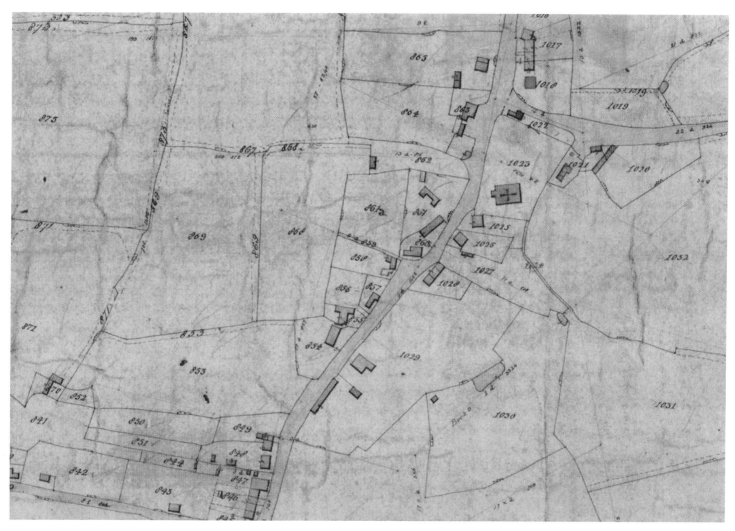

48 Extract from a tithe map of Billingshurst, West Sussex. The church (1023) is marked with a cross.

of the church and churchyard, roads, apprenticing youngsters and providing for the poor, and at a time when there were no addresses and the range of surnames in a settlement was more limited, those mentioned in the array of such information were often identified by the name of their house or farm. This can be of immense value, as those names can often be traced from a medieval owner or occupier and still feature in some form on modern Ordnance Survey maps.

One of the best starting points for those who want to investigate houses in both settlements and scattered locations are the parish **tithe maps and schedules (48)**. As a result of legislation in 1836, over the following ten years every parish was mapped, all its features (houses, fields, roads) numbered, and those numbers presented in a schedule which listed landlords, owners and occupiers. Many record offices have now digitised this information, making it easier to access and manipulate, with a little practice. From this point a house can be located, sometimes linked to an estate and tracked forwards through the census returns, which survive every ten years from 1841, are handwritten in varying degrees of legibility, and can be viewed on fiche. Many county offices also hold records produced for the purposes of land taxation, usually from the 1780s to 1832 and on film or fiche. These too are handwritten and give owners and occupants, and in some cases house or farm names, and it is sometimes possible to work backwards year by year from the tithe records.

Record offices will also have collections of other historic maps, the most readily accessible being the first three editions of the Ordnance Survey, between c.1875 and c.1911. These can illustrate changes to a house plan, as well as the way a settlement has grown and how its roads and pattern of fields may have been altered.

Another obvious question to ask is whether the building is 'Listed'. After World War 2 a national initiative was launched to identify and catalogue buildings that were part of the country's heritage. In spite of increases in knowledge and several re-classifications, the quality and accuracy of the entries in these lists are variable, but they can be a 'first way in' to identifying a building that looks interesting. There are over 5,000 'listed buildings' in the South Downs National Park, which includes grand houses like Arundel Castle, Petworth and Goodwood, and many churches. Below are examples for two of the buildings illustrated in this guide; note the different years of record.

CHESIL STREET (East Side) No 1
1950. II GV*
(Old St Peter's Rectory). (Cheese Rouse). Dated 1459 but probably early C16. 2 storeys. Two gables to road front. Timber-framed with plaster infilling; upper part over-sails brick ground floor. Carved barge-boards to gable ends. Projecting porch with carved head. C17 panelling in interior. Modern windows on either aide of doorway. Tiled roof.

JEVINGTON Filching Manor
1966 GII
L-shaped building. The original portion is a C15 timber-framed and close-studded building of wealden type with the first floor of the ends jettied and the eaves of the centre supported on curved brackets. Tiled roof. Casement windows. Several original windows with wooden mullions. Later wing to south-west.

49 A good example of a 'continuous-jetty' urban building in Petersfield, with an uneven ridge-line, close-studding and some visible arch-bracing.

Three Case Studies

Three work-in-progress examples can show how documentary sources can be searched and linked with buildings to give a more rounded picture. These examples have been chosen as two of the buildings are accessible to the public and one is in an urban setting that is easily visible. **The Clergy House at Alfriston (50)** began life as a classic Wealden with a single bay hall, which has been clearly re-modelled and extended, although according to David Martin it has constructional details that suggest the carpenter was unfamiliar with the style. One way to begin documentary investigations is to build up a 'time line', at first using easily available information, such as the entries for Alfriston in the Domesday Book (published by Phillimore, county by county) which show how much the place was divided between landowners. At least two local estates and property belonging to other estates are still recorded in later centuries. The National Trust website lists seven key years in the life of the building, although the structural points, such as the date of the building and when its windows were glazed, have to be taken as approximate. A point well made is the caution that although it was called the Clergy House, it would have been unusual for celibate (unmarried) priests to live there before the Reformation when the parish was being served by the canons of

Time Lines

These are a way of listing (in date order and note form) any information that may relate to a building and its owners and/or occupants, found while trawling through a whole variety of sources, both printed and original. A number of printed sources can be found in the 'local history' sections of larger libraries, and it is becoming easier to locate sources on-line. Jotting down information in this way is an exercise that can be started before actually visiting a building and helps to set it into its historical context. As the information builds up it can provide clues and suggest pathways for more in-depth research. At first sight these notes look daunting and complicated, but they provide the vital documentary clues to understanding a property. So do persevere when you read them here!

Most record offices now have on-line catalogue sites that will give summaries of each piece of information and a reference number which can be quoted when making a visit to see documents 'in the flesh'. It is most important to get into the habit of noting where you found the information. However much you are sure you will never forget, it is only too easy to do so. Just some (but not all) of these sources are included to illustrate this point, such as VCH (Victoria County History), SAC (Sussex Archaeological Collections), SRS (Sussex Record Society volumes), FF (Feet of Fines or property records in SRS), TNA (The National Archives), SNQ (Sussex Notes and Queries), ESRO (East Sussex Record Office), WSRO (West Sussex Record Office).

50 After Bayleaf at Singleton, the Clergy House at Alfriston is one of the best-known (and accessible) Wealdens, built c.1400. Details of the building suggest it was built by someone who was struggling with an unfamiliar style of construction (info. D. Martin). It was the first house bought by the National Trust, in 1896.

Michelham Priory, and for much of its life the house was rented out as a source of income. The name reflected the *ownership* of the property, that it belonged to the clergy of the parish, although after the Reformation under Elizabeth I, some of the married clergy may have lived there, but even Hugh Walker, who was vicar for over 30 years, moved out when his family became too cramped.

To get a 'feel' for the place, ferret out any local histories or guides, while treating them with caution and noting their publication dates, for research goes on and ideas change. Two were originally published in 1970 (Piper, Boyd) and another has been recently published (Juliet Clarke, 2011). There are both printed church guides, and the Sussex Parish Churches and Alfriston websites. Looking at the church is essential, for much of it will be contemporary with the historic buildings in its parish, and its structure and the beliefs it represented were of the greatest significance in the lives of their inhabitants, who would have worshipped there. In the case of the Clergy House with its direct link to the church and parish, this is even more important, as it tells of the connection with Michellham Priory, whose origins and history are covered in the *Victoria County History* (Sussex) vol. 2.

A trawl of the volumes of the Sussex Archaeological Society and their *Notes and Queries*, using the index volumes as a guide, makes it possible to construct lists of rectors and vicars for Alfriston, as well as supplying relevant local material like the Star Chamber account (1624). The clergy database on-line can provide biographical detail about local clergy, generally from the late 16th century, while certain volumes of the Sussex Record Society are generally useful, such as vols. 7, 11 & 23 (Feet of Fines or property records), vol. 41 (Wills A-C), vol. 56 (1524/5 taxation records), vol. 77 & 82 (1785 land tax), vol. 78 (diocesan surveys) and supplement the more specific references.

The catalogues of the National Archive (TNA) and in this case the East Sussex Record Office (ESRO) at The Keep give summarised information and point in the direction of original documents, such as leases and wills. The 1560 Exchequer record showed that after c.1548, income from Alfriston vicarage had been directed to be used as a 'pension pot' for a poor priest, probably to the dismay of the vicar. Resorting to British History Online brought up a history of St Augustine Pappey, founded in 1442 to care for up to 60 old and infirm priests, but suppressed with other fraternities under Edward VI, in the drive to Protestantism. It then seems ironic that in 1628 the income from both rectory and vicarage became part of the endowment of the Henry Smith Charity, to provide for needy clergymen. A biography of Henry Smith (1549–1628) was published in 2015, expanding upon the little that had previously been known, and his charity is still operating today. Moreover, at ESRO there is a collection of the trustees' leases of the rectory and vicarage from 1682 to 1813, the summaries giving an interesting list of local names which need further examination, as do related wills.

As the time line builds up, the information collected points towards other lines of investigation and other sources that may be relevant, and raises questions to be explored. Was it Michelham Priory who built the Clergy House or a local carpenter-cum-developer with an eye to the main chance? A Michelham priest was taking a service in 1419, and another was 'acting as vicar' in 1524, but were they actually living there? How was the building used over the centuries, and when and why did occupancy change? Exactly what was leased in the 17th and 18th centuries? There may be more information in the parish records. Some of the references may go towards explaining when and why the house was adapted and changed, remembering that the 19th century restoration removed the first floor inserted into the open hall when a chimney was built. The Clergy House draft 'time line' is shown in abbreviated note form and only some of the source references are listed, although this should be done for every entry. Note that specific references to the Clergy House are much more frequent from 1618 onwards.

ALFRISTON CLERGY HOUSE TIME LINE

1086 Domesday record

Alciston 100

Gilbert holds 1 hide from the Count [*Robert of Mortain*] in *Alvricestone*
at revenue

Ælfric held it as freehold

Land for 1 plough

Now 1 smallholder

Value before 1066, later & now 8s

In *Alvricestone* itself **Ranulf holds 1 hide from the Count**

Ralph ½ hide, William ½ hide, Ralph 1 hide Walter 2 hides

5 hides in total It answers for as much

Leofwin, Alfwold, Alnoth & Godwin held this land as freehold

Land for 5 ploughs Now in lordship 3½ ploughs

2 villagers and 6 smallholders plough the half

Total value before 1066 20s now 54s

1071 Battle Abbey founded land within 1½ mile radius, Alciston etc

1094 Battle Abbey church consecrated

1229 VCH 2 Michelham founded by Gilbert of L'aigle, lord of the Rape of Pevensey

1239 SAC 57.174 Agnes wid/o Wm Montague held advowson

1288 Thos de Montague rector

1317 Wm de Mari, rector

1352 Peter de Hoo, rector

1372 Rd Suggeworth, rector

1385 Wm Everle, rector

1396 Advowson: Bp Chichester > Michelham (vicarage to be endowed)

? c1400 Clergy House constructed ?

1400 Jn Carlton, vicar

1401 FF2705 Wm & Jul Hendeman to Wm Everle clerk, Jn Carleton chaplain etc: mess, 50a, rents

1403 FF2739 Jn & Agatha Heghlond to Jn Carleton chaplain: mess, 1a. Was this the Clergy House ?

1416 (Piper 1970) Robert Nevyll **vicar**

1419 SRS 36.141 Dom Robert, chaplain, celebrating in Alfriston church

1460 Jn Wetlee & Wm Calmoure **vicars**

1450 Jack Cade's rebellion: 17 local men pardoned

1517 (Piper 1970) Jn Burrell, clerk, 'from Alfriston' convicted of stealing horse at Rye'

1524 One canon acting as vicar (visitation)

1524/5 SRS 56.116 Tax return inc. Jn & Rd Elphicke under Alfriston

1535 Valor Ecc Alfriston church valued @ £16.13.4

1543/58 Rd Cresweller vicar

1546/7 Dissolution of monasteries

1560 TNA E 135/1/22/1 Assessment of Alfriston vicarage (Sussex) and its tithable value for **Richard Bagge, clerk**, pursuant to the discharge of a pension payable out of that vicarage

TNA E 135/1/22/139 request to take bonds from Richard Bagge, priest, to discharge the Queen of the annual pension of 4 marks payable to George Strowger out of the hospital called [St. Augustine] Pappey in the city of London, which is to be paid out of the vicarage of Alfriston . . .

1563 Non resident vicar; no curate

1568 Thos Banister vicar

1572 Dionis Hurst vicar (whose tongue scraper & earpick was found in 1849)

1585 Jn Dobson vicar

1586 SAC 53.2 *'The chancell is in decaye the falte is in our rector Jn Rootes'* [of Maresfield]

1593 Hugh Minshull als Walker vicar

1618 Chatsworth mss [ESRO SAS-CP/11/8/351]
John Deward survey (Cuckmere Levels) names Clergy House as 'Vicarage house Mr Hue Walker'

1624 SNQ 2.183 A long account of proceedings in Star Chamber whereby two of vicar's seven children, Christophilus & Hugh, illegally pressed into military service, had to be released by a bribe (from their father) of 13s 4d apiece

1626–1640 Thos Tyroe vicar (3 wives buried)

1627 'Dog' Smith charity inc. impropriate rectory: for needy clergymen

1635 WSRO Ep II/17/154 glebe terrier

1676 ESRO AMS 5882/1 glebe terrier (draft)

1671–1709 Robt Nurth, vicar

1673 Thos Malthus vicar

1682–1813 SAS FA952ff Henry Smith's charity trustees: rectory & parsonage

1682 Lease to Jn **Elphick**, mercer, lt Thos **Chowne**, Wm Adams & Thos Markewicke

1688 TNA PROB 11/393/75 Will of Thomas Chowne of Alfriston

1702 ESRO PBT 1/1/45/27 Will of Jn Elphick, mercer

1708 Lease to **Wm Gyles**, late Thos Tourll

1711 Wm Gyles > s Wm

1723 Occupied by Wm Giles

1724 ESRO PBT 1/1/51/329A Will of Wm Giles gent

1724 *'The Mansion house & barne in good repair'* (Wm Barttelott from 1715)

1735 Lease to Wm Batchelor & Wm Lee

1753 Lease to Eleanor Batchelor, widow

1769 & '76 Lease to Jn Rason, Rd King, Rd Newman, farmers

1790 Lease to **Thomas Harben**, Lewes banker

c1790 Converted to two labourers' cottages (Boyd 1970/95)

1812 Lease to Thos Harben, Berwick House

1813 Lease to **Thos Cooper**

1832 SAS GA 1341/5 (In correspondence) patronage of vicarage returned to bishop who offered it to Mr Smith [Chas Bohun Smith] a relative of his first wife. Smith was alarmed at the condition of parish and maintained a new house was essential, possibly using funds from Queen Anne's Bounty

1842 Tithe map

1883 ESRO OBIT/1/47/216 death of Harriet Coates at the Old Vicarage

1890 proposal to demolish 'very dilapidated used as labourers' cottage for some time'

1892 ESRO ACC8859/5/1 Printed appeal by Rev Beynon (DECD 1898) for the preservation of the Old Clergy House

1896 Purchase by National Trust

For the second example we travel westwards towards **Sullington**, one of those places under the Downs where the access off the Storrington road leads to the farm, its yard, the small parish church, and little else. Both parish and manor extended north of the main road, and the manor included outlying land-holdings to the west of Horsham, partly hidden within the 30 pigs' worth of woodland listed in 1086. Starting the time line with Domesday highlights how different the settlement appears by comparison with Alfriston, being nearly all in the hands of one tenant-in-chief, William de Braose, lord of Bramber Rape. The clue to the nature of this collection of buildings lies in the present name – **Manor Farm** – suggesting that, at the very least, this was the site of the 'home farm' of the manor of Sullington. In this case it was examination of the building and trying to understand its development that directed documentary research, so a simple plan of a very complex building is included, along with the way in which it was described **(51)**.

The evidence of the building established several things: the earliest survival was high-status and probably dating from the end of the 1200s; it was substantially

PLAN Sullington (51)

Description notes

This house at Sullington is part of a group which includes the church, two large barns, a granary and/or dovecote, cart shed and other farm buildings. It is made up of three units, with tiled roofs and elevations in a mixture of stone and brick; wings aligned east/west are linked by a north/south central range. This central range contains the remnants of a truss from an early building on the site, characterised by roll moulding on the underside of part of a brace and the remains of, or evidence for, parallel bracing halved to the posts. The plates that extend south from this truss have no evidence of framing on their undersides. In the roof space there is a later wattle-and-daub partition above this truss, heavily sooted to the north, where a large stack has since been inserted.

South from this truss the roof has been reconstructed with crown-posts of which one remains intact (X), braced down to the tie and southwards to the collar purlin. The collars are inconsistently halved to the north and south of the rafters. The roof is fairly consistently sooted. The roofs over the wings are both of staggered butt-purlin construction, the southern wing also having dropped ties, with evidence that the rooms at both ground and first floor had plastered ceilings, possibly decorative. The northern wing has unusual wind-bracing above the purlins. Both wings appear to have contained two room spaces at each level, of unequal sizes. The northern wall of the southern wing, where it abuts the linking range, is of noticeably thick masonry, and at ground level (east) is a stone doorway (D) with an arched head.

Comment

The remnant contained within the central range must be of a high-status open hall, and is probably the low-end spere (screen) truss of a construction with simple collared rafters. The lack of evidence for framing under the horizontal plates, stone doorway and earlier photographs, all suggest strongly it was double-aisled and had a stone solar block to the south. The sooted partition remains from an intermediate phase of smoke control, predating the large chimney stack. The 10-bay aisled barn is particularly notable and its staggered butt-purlin roof with raking struts is comparable with the wings of the house. The sequential carpenters' marks show that it was constructed in one campaign, using a good proportion of recycled material, particularly in the eastern bays.

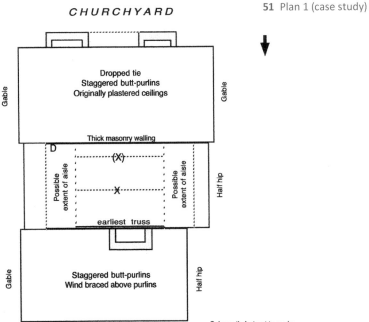

CHURCHYARD

51 Plan 1 (case study)

Dropped tie
Staggered butt-purlins
Originally plastered ceilings

Gable

Gable

Thick masonry walling

D

Possible extent of aisle

(X)

x

Possible extent of aisle

Half hip

earliest truss

Staggered butt-purlins
Wind braced above purlins

Gable

Half hip

Schematic but not to scale

County History of Sussex, vol. 6 pt. 2 (1986) and this provides a framework for any further investigations. There is also the work of Joan Ham, a local historian, and her publications and transcriptions of Sullington manorial records can be found in the West Sussex Record Office. These establish the lords of the manor from the mid 1200s as the de Covert family, although there is a hint that this was the result of a marriage. In the early 1200s a de Covert from Chaldon married the daughter of Reynold Aguillon – which raises the possibility that they preceded the de Coverts at Sullington; it may be Sir William Covert who is buried beneath the damaged

reconstructed just over a hundred years later; then substantially rebuilt in the 16th and 17th centuries. It must have been the principal dwelling of the manor, and centre of its administration, occupied by its lord when he was present, or when he was absent, by his bailiff/steward; a true 'manor house'.

Fortunately Sullington is covered by a comparatively recent article in the *Victoria*

52 Sketch (case study)
Barn at Sullington.
One of two significant barns, this one awaits restoration. Barns were built on the same principles as framed houses, and can be easier to see and understand.

SULLINGTON W.Sx   Farmyard and Church 14 July

53 Sketch (case study) Farmyard and church. This illustrates the integration often found between historic manor house, church, farmyard and its buildings.

54 Sullington Manor Farm, illustrating the three elements of central hall and two cross-wings. The church is to the left, just out of the picture.

effigy in the church. This is where articles in the *Sussex Archaeological Collections*, taken with Keats-Rohan on '*Domesday Descendants*' provide valuable background on both de Coverts and Aguillons. Unwinding this thread makes it possible to go back to the first Aguillon recorded in Sussex; Geoffrey d'Aguillon was chancellor of the diocese in the late 1100s, while Manasser was holding land from the Earl of Arundel, tenant-in-chief of the adjoining Rape, Bramber.

Apart from being mentioned in correspondence between the Bishop of Chichester and his steward, Simon de Senliz, Reynold Aguillon is described as '*a man of some standing, as from 1220 to 1226 he was bailiff, or steward, of the honor of Arundel, and in 1225 he was employed by the king to arrest all ships carrying corn in the ports of Kingston, Wodering, and Horemue [Chichester]*'.

Because Sullington farm was the manor house it appears in three surveys – after the death of Roger de Covert in 1297, among the possessions of the Earl of Arundel in 1399, and again in 1582 – all implying a house where courts were held. And there are courts for which some records survive. This is underlined by the record of a grant in 1313, writing of '*the grantor's court at Sullington*' where courts were held every three weeks.

These and other references all confirm the status of the earliest building: almost certainly that it was the house mentioned in 1297, and that it served the de Coverts until their line failed in the 1360s. It was then taken over by the Earls of Arundel who used its income in 1395 to provide funds for their newly-founded 'hospital' or 'Maison Dieu' – a retirement home for 20 poor men. This is probably when there was a complete overhaul and the roof was rebuilt with crown-posts, making it more profitable for the college to lease out. This was the second time Sullington had been closely linked with an ecclesiastical

55 (case study) Open hall-house in South Harting with 'butterfly bracing' and side-purlins, which showed how residents here looked westwards for inspiration. The open hall was either adapted to a continuous jetty or had an original gallery, another feature found more often in Hampshire.

foundation. In the 1240s the church tithes had been granted to Sele Priory at Beeding, and after a bitter disagreement the Dean and Chapter drafted a compromise, which was agreed. In the 'feeding frenzy' of land acquisition after the dissolution of the monasteries, Sullington was sold to Edward Shelley of Warminghurst. The subsequent major work on the house must have been carried out while the Shelleys

were landlords, and Horsham Museum Society has published work by S. Djabri on the Shelley properties.

Published entries in the Tompkins diary, the land tax and parish registers show that the Fullers were followed by the Hamptons and then by Henry Hardwicke, who remained as tenant until his death, c.1867 **(51, 52, 53, 54)**.

Fowlers Buck, The Street, South Harting

(Proportional but not to scale; approximate imperial measurements)

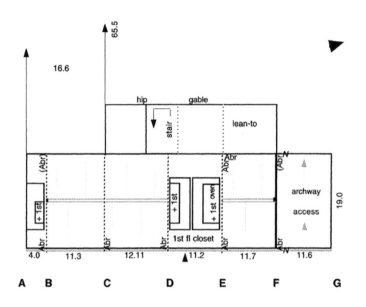

The final study is from the far west of West Sussex, close to Hampshire, and is a private house on the main street in **South Harting,** called **Fowlers Bucke (55)**. A written record with a simple plan was made in 2009, as part of a general survey of Harting houses, so the plan and a written description are given here. Characteristics of its construction suggested it was built in the second half of the 1400s, and could

be compared with a style better known in Hampshire; an open **(56) plan** hall but with a continuous jetty frontage, created by carrying a gallery across the front of the open hall.

It is clear from the evidence of the building that it was a house of considerable quality, but the first conjunction of the named owner and property is not found until the

1650 will of Thomas Fowler, leaving '*the house called the Bucke*' to his son John; Thomas may have inherited the property from his grandfather, Richard Gervis also Rablis. The name does not necessarily mean that it was built as an inn, although there are documents such as that of 1555 linking a Fowler of Harting with the tavern trade – the Fowlers seem to have moved north from the coast. The series of alterations to achieve the house as it appeared in 1650 can be briefly summarised. About the mid 1500s a partition was inserted at D to channel the smoke from the hearth, and this may have been in conjunction with a smoke hood which was obliterated when the chimney stacks were built in, either together or in sequence. The chimney stacks would have been built in at the end of the 1500s, and the painted decoration seems to have been contemporary. In the early 1600s the gabled wing was built to contain a stair, which was subsequently moved, and in the late 1600s the attics were created by ceiling over the first floor rooms. The probate records with their references to glass and wainscot (wall-panelling) illustrate what a fine property it was by 1676.

SULLINGTON MANOR FARM TIME LINE

1086 Domesday record

Arundel Rape Easewrithe 100

    Robert *(le Sauvage)* holds 1 virgate in *SILLINTONE*

    Wulfward held it from King Edward

    1 villager with ½ plough

    The value is & was 2s

Bramber Rape Steyning 100

    William *(de Braose)* himself holds *SEMLINTUN*

    Wulfward held it from King Edward

    Then it answered for 9 hides now for 4

    3 virgates of this land are in Arundel Rape

    Land for 7 ploughs In lordship 3 ploughs

    20 villagers and 14 smallholders with 6 ploughs

    1 mill at 6s; meadow 6 acres; **woodland 30 pigs**

    Value before 1066 £9; later and now £8

1166 SAC 79.45ff Manasser Aguillon holding 2 knights' fees from Earl of Arundel

c1229 SAC 3 Reynold Aguillon (decd 1230/3) mentioned in correspndence of Simon de Senliz, steward to Bp Chichester before 1230 Mary dau/o Reynold Aguillon m **Wm Couvert of Chaldon**

1242 William de Covert held 2 kts' fees (at Sullington & Broadbridge Heath)

1235 Sele chartulary. 15 Tithes of Sullington church confirmed to **Sele priory**

1247 Sele 33 Dispute re tithes owing from Sullington (rector = Sir Roger)

1296 Tax SRS 10   *with Thakeham*   *inc*   *Rog de Covert*

1297 IPM Rog de Covert   TNA C133/83/19   SAC 46.174

Court with gardens	**3s 4d**
112a arable	37s 4d
10a meadow	10s
an enclosed meadow	4s
Pasture & heath	9s
2 water mills & 1 windmill	40s
rents of free tenants	54s 2d
rents of naifs	£4.4.3
work of customary tenants	60s
advowson of church	10 marks
Total £15.2.1 besides the advowson	

1312 FF1331 Master Wm de Alneto with Jn & Isabel Covert (**manor & advowson**)

1313 Add Mss 256 Grant

For 20s. and annual rent of 5s. 11½d. and suit of **court from three weeks to three weeks at the grantor's court at Sullington** John de Covert, s. & heir of Roger de Covert, kt,. to Daniel ate Forwelde and s. Adam, and the heirs and assigns of Adam

1315 FF1382 Wm de Alneto parson of Sullington & Robert de Alneto with Jn & Isabel Covert

1327 Tax   22 payers inc Jn de Covert

1332 Tax   24 payers inc Jn de Covert

1336 FF1839 Jn (de Weston) rector of Sullington > Jn & Margt de Covert (**manor**)

1351 FF2096 reversion to Earl of Arundel after dec of Margaret & s-in-law Baldwin Moigne (**manor & church**)

1366-7 ACM1864 Accounts

    SRS 45 Margaret, wife of Jn de Covert, buried in the church

1379 reversion > E of Arundel

1379/80 TNA E135/15/3 **College of canons at Arundel** founded (at St Nicholas)

1395 Hospital of the Holy Trinity (Maison Dieu) founded in Arundel Sullington among endowments (inc property west of Horsham)

1399 FitzAlan (of Arundel) survey

Here is a garden worth 3s 4d

Also 140a arable worth £3.10.0 and 100a pasture worth £1

Also £11.13.0 in assised rents

The court brings in 6s 8d and the pasture in the park *(at Broadbridge)* is worth £1

Total £18

The demesne can support 2 farm horses, 20 oxen, 20 cows, 300 wethers and 150 ewes

1425 Add Mss 48269 Court Roll of Sullington

1438–40 MF1650 Court Book

1544 Dissolution: Hospital > Henry, Earl of Arundel > Edw **Shelley** of Warminghurst acquired Sullington

1554 decd Edward Shelley > grandson Henry

1555–59 Add Mss 246   Manor of Sullington   Court roll

1582 ACM Survey by Rd Benten (Ham 106)

    Demesne inc: howse, gates, garden & orchard

owlde mylle garden lying by ye Chaunterye garden wch I bought of Nich Wase sheepe downe of 400 sheepe

      Pasture 282ac 3r

      Arable 145½ ac

      Meadows 46a 3½ r

      Total 363a 1½ r

1621 Henry Shelley of Sullington; decd 1623 > 2 moieties; 'mansion house' at Sullington

1st pt Djabri p23ff Warneford > Shelley > White > Arnold > Shelley of Lewes > D'Albiac > Carew-Gibson

1767 2nd pt Shelley > > Sr John Shelley

1741 Tompkins Diary SAC 71.19

sold for Jn Shelley 8 walnut trees @ 8d p ft growing near the Woodhouse & Workhouse at Sullington farm

1767 Tompkins SAC 71.13 Eleanor & Thos Fuller, lessees of Jn Shelley

1785 SRS 82 Land Tax Thomas Fuller, tenant of John Shelley

1773–1782 Thomas & Elizabeth Fuller had 4 children

1789 Sullington Farm sold to Ld Egremont

1822–31 John Hampton, tenant, had 6 children, 3 of whom died young

1839–53 Henry & Mary Hardwicke had 7 children

1840T Sullington Homestead   Wyndham (Petworth) Henry Hardwicke

1907 Heck family from Dorset Albert & son Bernard decd 1952

1952 SP491, 969, 1894 Kittle

PLAN FOWLERS BUCKE (56)

Description notes

Fowlers Bucke is situated south of the White Hart in South Harting, on the west side of and parallel with the street. Its tiled roof is gabled and both ends and the front elevation are plastered with a continuous jetty of six bays, the northernmost of which is an archway access. There are additions to the rear elevation in stone with brick trim, the oldest of which is two-storey, partly framed, gabled and with replacement barge-boards and pendant. A Sun fire insurance plaque is dated 1710. A brick-built malthouse extends west from the southern end.

The timbering is of very heavy scantling and there is a high standard of finish. Girders are all stop-chamfered as are the joists in CD & EF on which the carpenter's assembly numbers are clear. Mid-ties are stop-chamfered to the girders. Two large inglenook hearths with timber bressumers are set on stone bases at D & E, with the holes for spit jack fixing on both and a bread oven at E. BC is panelled with moulding to the top and sides of each panel and a plain lower edge chamfer. There is a smaller plastered hearth off-centre within AB.

The first floor is reached by means of a dog-leg stair within a rear projection with a surviving length of nicely finished hand-rail with turned balusters. A large coloured glass panel has been introduced in the walling of an adjacent gabled projection. At first floor posts with jowled profiles are just visible along the front elevations and there are arch-braces or mortice evidence where indicated (Abr). The eaves plates extended north of F and have edge-halved scarf joints. Ceiling heights are varied, being noticeably raised within CD. The ties at C & E have roll-moulding along their northern faces with one early run-out end still surviving. There are first-floor hearths throughout; at D there is a four-centred arch to the hearth with painted spandrel decoration that extends over onto the flanking stud. Within CD is evidence for a remarkable painted scheme over timbers and plastering with drawn outlines infilled predominantly with blue. The roof is constructed with clasped side-purlins and 'fan' trusses C to F. At C the collar has been cut for access to the southern attic space, where the roof has been re-constructed from C and is quite clean. There is a daubed partition to apex at D, which is heavily sooted on the whole of its northern face, but the soot-staining extends over the roof timbers throughout, except where specified.

There is a wealth of documents and a series of complex deeds on the Bucke and the properties to each side, which illustrate how difficult it may be to disentangle a single property by ownerships and 'abutments'. The first positive reference to 'John Fowler's inn called the Bucke' is in 1683, 'south-west of the Vine House'. By 1714, when the grocer John Luff died, he left to his wife Elizabeth 'the house and garden late Fowlers', but in 1767 the Bucke was the Horse and Groom, and in 1778 'now the White Hart Inn'. No structure in the present White Hart building pre-dates c.1600. By 1785 it seems to have come into the hands of the Wilds, a local brewing family, and all or part was still operating as an inn in the tenancy of William Peacock. In 1831 however, it is described as *'previously the Buck Inn later Horse and Groom **used for many years as a private house'**. Ten years later the tithe map schedule distinguishes between The White Hart and widow Wild's Fowlers Bucke, which was firmly in two occupations in 1894.

HARTING FOWLERS BUCKE TIME LINE

1524 tax Thos **Fowler** (Aldingbourne) Jn Fowler (Lyminster)

1555 TNA Wine Licence: **Geo Fowler** als Myller of Harting, tavern for 10 years

Copy of wine licence: issued by Q Mary & K Philip to George Fowler alias Myller of Harting 18th July 1555 (sourced as PRO S.C66/905 IC/323)

1556 Will: Geo Fowler

1587 Will of John Rablis also Gervis inc. son Richard, & 2 daughters

1638 Will of Richard Gervis also Rablis inc. grandson Thomas Fowler

1650 Will & Prob Inv Thos Fowler th'elder (**inc the Bucke**) 21.330 glass and wainscot in hall, parlour & chamber over hall to wife Barbery **The Bucke;** house, stable, orchard, part of barn next stable ?life interest to son Thomas table, great chest, wainscot, glass in chamber over hall, ditto in hall and parlour, part barn by John Kent's garden

1675 House & malthouse occ Thos Heth (Thos Fowler > s Wm) **House called the Bucke   (Thos > s John)**

1676 Will of Thomas Fowler to son Thomas items in parlour, wainscot, glass, bed in little chamber, 2 in great loft

1683 Feoffment: mess, tenmt, dwelling, smith's shop etc 'the Wine House & ½ a' Hen Kent with Thos Meredith, Harting fellmonger

ref Vine House occ Rd Kent adj **SW Jn Fowler's Inn called The Buck** N Jn Hodges dwelling

1684 Feoffmt: messuage, tenement, smith's shop, orchard, b'side known as the Wine House & ¼ a Land adj **SW on Jn Fowler's Inn called the Buck**
N hse of Jn Hedges
Thos Meredith with Thos Geale, Harting innholder

1703 **The Buck Inn** (Jn Luff from Wm Fowler) **built brewhse & stable**
. . . adj house & gdn of Rd Scardefield
Luff sold 1 rood betw > Scardefield with provisos

1711 House & malthouse (Rd Scardefield maltster, mortgage > Rd Watson)

1714 Will & Prob Inv   **Jn Luffe, grocer** 31.455
Hse & garden late Fowlers > w Eliz for life

1767 Add Mss 12187 Lease **Buck Inn now Horse & Groom lt Rd Lever now Rd Pink**
Jn Hounsome, Lond. linen draper s&h/o Jn lt of Funtington s&h/o Jn of Emsworth by w Eliz née Luff (cf W 1714) with Jn Blackmore

1778 Lease ½ mess, dwelling, malthse, stables etc **fmly Buck Inn now White Hart Innn**   fmly occ Thos Geale now Dan Parr
Ant Aldridge & w Susannah (d & coh/o Thos Geale) with neph Wm Aldridge

1785LT	Geo Mullings & Co	Jn Lever	land & malthouse	£9
	Jn Blackmore	Thos Blackmore	hse, gdn & shop	£3
	"	self	"	£5
	Jn Wild & Co	**Wm Peacock**	**hse, gdn & malthouse**	**£8**
	. . . . . .			
	Scardfield Jn	self	hse & shop	£2
	Jn Miller	"	"	£1
	Rd Pink[1]	"	"	£1.10
	Thos Chitty	"	"	£1.10

1791 Sr Hen Featherstonhaugh with Jn (W1792) & Mary **WILD**
  S property with Thos G(e)ale's dwelling (see 1778)
  N gdn/orchard of Edw and/or Wm Ruff
  Fmly occ Jn Pannell (?butcher[2]) then Jn Lake, surgeon, then Jn Wild

1801 Lease: ⅓ of above occ Wm Peacock
  Mary Wild wid (d/o Thos Geale) with Wm Aldridge carpenter &
  Thos Curtis surg (trust)
1831 Add Mss 12189/90 Lease **Mess previously Buck Inn later**
  Horse & Groom used for many years as private house
  ref 1816 W Jn Blackmore (2)
  1830 dec Eliz Blackmore quitclaimed Jas & Ann Ewens
  trustee Wm Curtis surgeon for Jn Blackmore (3)
  ref Geo Wild & Sarah (née Blackmore; Jn 2)
1840T (from sth of White Hart)
  375 Wm Wild   self   corner plot

377	Wm Curtis	self	
378	Hect Cornthwaite	Jn/Geo Temple	The White Hart
379	**Wid Wild**	**self**	**Fowlers Bucke**
			(+malthse)
380	Wid Lever	self	

1894 12209 Further mortg: **Mess fmly Buck Inn lt Horse & Groom**
  (Lever > Pink > Jn Blackmore > Eliz Blackmore > Jn Blackmore)
  many years 2 private houses (Sar Wild, Mrs Pay)
  then 3 (Wiggins, Pettitt, Oliver)
  now 4 (Geo Mundy & tenants)

1906 12227 dec Jn Donald Blackmore of White Hart, lic.vict.
  ref 6 freehold cotts since sold
1976/7 Restoration by Kenneth & Cynthia Bacon: discovery of painted
  scheme, and shoe with pack of drilled bones next to hearths

[1]1705.30.773 Rd Pink, carpenter, w Mary exec house in SH > underage childr Jn, Rd, Thos, Mary at 21 to be sold & divided betwe them & wid
[2]Wills 1815 48.48 (butcher) & 1829 50.149 (blacksmith)

These examples have just touched on the challenges that can arise even when one seems to have both an interesting building and lots of documentary references, and hopefully it also conveys some of the fascination of both looking at buildings and trying to discover their stories.

Be Your Own House Detective

Please remember, that apart from those buildings that are open to the public, houses in the South Downs National Park are private homes and should be treated with respect, even though owners may

58 This shows the very distinct differences between two building periods, with tile-hanging concealing a wooden framework, and later the use of 'burnt headers' in a chequer pattern. From a house in Barcombe.

well regard themselves as 'temporary custodians' **(57-62)**.

What outside clues can help towards understanding the history of a house?

Try to work out the ground PLAN. Without exception these buildings were originally only single-pile – that is, originally one room wide – and rectangular. The easiest way to gain additional space, without making a house unreasonably long, was by adding wings at right angles to the original rectangle, as well as single-storey 'lean-tos' with sloping 'catslide' roofs.

57 English bond brickwork above a coursed stone plinth.

Summary of medieval plan types:

- 3 or more bays with aisles
- 4 bay 'norm' of 2 bay hall flanked by floored ends (service & solar)
- High (solar) & low (service) ends usually of 1 bay
- Cross entry or passage at low end of hall, or within service
- 2 bay hall + single floored end (3 bay)
- Single bay hall flanked by floored ends (3 bay)
- Single bay hall + single floored end (2 bay)
- Cross-wing (2-5 bays) in place of either or both floored ends

59 The proportions, gabled roof and pattern of framing suggest that the George & Dragon at Houghton was built with a chimney. The 'wavy' ridge line shows it was built before ridge boards were introduced, c.1750. Earlier, it was known simply as The George, and in 1614 the tenant acquired a wine licence.

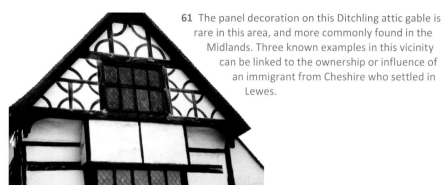

61 The panel decoration on this Ditchling attic gable is rare in this area, and more commonly found in the Midlands. Three known examples in this vicinity can be linked to the ownership or influence of an immigrant from Cheshire who settled in Lewes.

60 A straight vertical edge in English bond brickwork, which should alert the observer to the probability that it reveals a constructional change.

62 The end wings on this Barlavington house have the queen strut trusses of side-purlin roofs, and the whole has been extensively stone faced and infilled. The large curved braces at the left are the clue that the core of the house is actually pre-1500.

63 This house in Sutton illustrates regular square framing with brick infill, some laid in herring-bone fashion, and the addition of an outshot with catslide roof.

Look for any visible FRAMING as the patterns can help to to judge the age and dimensions. Timbers tended to be heavier in older buildings, and braces to be longer. Panels can be large and rectangular with long, storey-high curved braces (Medieval) or smaller and squarer with half-height straight braces (Transitional & Post-medieval). Half-rounds producing circular patterns within a panel are unusual in Sussex and can sometimes be related to an owner who was an 'incomer'. Full height posts (or parts of them) can help you to decide the number and width of bays. Posts on the corner of a building can have distinctive shapes towards the top (jowls or rootstocks). The roof framing visible on a gable end may reveal the construction, that is, whether it has crown-posts or side-purlins (63, 64, 65).

Look at the shape and proportions of the ROOF. Does it end in hips, half-hips or gables? Is the roof deep in proportion to the height of the building? An irregular or 'wavy' ridge line suggests a house was built before 1750; until about that time each pair of rafters was simply tenoned together and pegged at the apex without a ridge board, so that over time the natural settlement of the building produced an uneven line. If you can see the ends of the rafters at eaves level, their shape – either heavy, rectangular and set on the flat (Medieval) or slender, square and on edge (Transitional & Post-medieval) – can be a clue to the age of the house, or reveal if the roof has been rebuilt.

Summary of roof types:

- Sans-purlin with early features from c.1230 (can persist later over humble dwellings)
- Crown struts without purlins (movement towards crown-post)
- Crown-post and central purlin (the medieval 'norm')
- Clasped side-purlin with queen struts and wind-braces
- Side-purlin with raking struts and wind-braces
- Butt-purlins and butt rafters

The position of **CHIMNEYS** in relation to the plan can sometimes be the clue to whether they are later insertions. Are they more or less central in a house with medieval proportions, so possibly inserted into an open hall? Are they at the end of a building – internal or external – so more likely to have been built with the house? The latter sometimes began as end smoke bays.

64 Post-medieval characteristics of regular square framed panels and half-height bracing in Steyning. The empty notches are where there were smaller studs.

65 The full-height bracing and long passing braces on the near corner hint at a medieval building in Steyning.

Look carefully at any **SOLID WALLING** for signs of change, such as straight edges where a house has been extended or where openings have been changed **(66, 67, 68)**. Stone facing can be in well-finished and shaped blocks, random rubble or even like crazy paving. Bricks are laid in different BONDS, can vary in colour and size, and brick under-building can reveal where a frame has been cut back. Differences in brickwork can also show whether it was introduced in stages as the frame deteriorated, or all at once, suggesting an owner could afford a complete 'makeover'. **FLINT** needed brick around the windows and on the corners, and could be used as a substitute for more expensive stone.

Look at the positions and shapes of **WINDOWS**. Have they been enlarged or moved? Are there any surviving wooden mullions, and are they on the front or back of the building? Do the windows open out sideways (casement) or slide sideways ('Yorkshire' sashes) or up and down (box sashes)? Small panes of glass and thick glazing bars are clues to earlier rather than later types. Blocked windows do not always indicate tax avoidance; they may have been used to produce a symmetrical arrangement, or it might be that the arrangement of internal space has been changed. Are the heads of the first-floor windows set lower than the eaves plates? This usually indicates a dropped tie roof construction.

Be very cautious about inscribed **DATES**. On ordinary houses anything before about 1600 is highly unusual and therefore suspect. Even with later dates, it is worth trying to work out exactly what is being dated – the whole house, or just an addition or alteration.

66 The Old Post Office at Tillington clearly shows the right-hand side to be an addition: the proportions and hipped roof to the left suggest something earlier than the Georgian brickwork might indicate. It contains a late medieval open-hall house, with an added post-medieval single-storey lean-to at the rear.

Glossary
(building and inventory terms)

Aisle – The side compartment of a house, hall or barn, separated from the main body of the building by an arcade

Bay – Portion of a framed building between full height upright supporting timbers
Smoke bay – short bay between two trusses closed at roof level to confine and channel smoke

Beam – Main horizontal timber
Axial – celing beam along length of house
Transverse – across the width of a house

Bedstedle – Wooden framework of a bed

Brace – Subsidiary timber, curved or straight, normally between horizontal and vertical members of a frame

Bressumer – a horizontal timber above a fireplace opening

Box frame – Construction in which roof trusses are carried on a frame composed of posts, tie-beams and wall plates

Carpenter's marks – Incised numerals or symbols used in prefabricated construction to indicate matching timbers

Chimney
Axial – rising from the ridge
Lateral – within or outside an external side wall
Gable – within or outside an end gable

Cruck – A pair of timbers, straight or curved, serving as the principals of a roof, and extending from at or near the apex of the roof to well down the side walls
Cruck framed – a building constructed with crucks, as opposed to box-framed

Dais beam – decorated beam at the mid-level of the partition at the upper end of a hall

Dormer – Projection from slope of a roof with its own roof

Dragon beam – Beam running diagonally across the ceiling of a room to support jetties on two adjacent sides of an upper floor

Firkin (virkin) – Barrel for 56lbs or 9 gallons

Gridirons – Barred metal grid for grilling meat or fish

Hall – traditional term for the main living area of a house
Open hall – open to the roof with an open hearth
Open hearth – Normally clear of the walls without chimney stack or hood above

Jetty – Cantilevered overhang of an upper storey or gable

Joist – a horizontal timber supporting a floor or carrying a ceiling

Jowl – Swelling of the inner face of the top of a wall post to accommodate housings for wall plate and tie-beam

Lobby entry – leading into a lobby on the side of an axial chimney, with doors to rooms each side

Louvre – Opening on the ridge of a roof for the escape of smoke from an open hearth

Mullion – Vertical member within a window opening; may be square in section set diagonally

Plate – Longitudinal timber set square to the ground on top of a wall or in a roof truss

Post – Substantial vertical timber usually forming part of the main framework
Crown-post – upright timber standing on a tie-beam supporting the collar purlin or crown plate
Queen post – paired posts set on a tie-beam and supporting plates or purlins

Pothooks & hangers – Hooks for attaching cooking pots to crane (hanger) over fire

Purlin (side) – Longitudinal timber set in the plane of the roof slope and supporting common rafters

Rafter – Inclined timber, usually one of a pair, supporting laths under a roof covering

Roof – Main roof forms are gabled, hipped & half-hipped

Catslide – covers one side of the main slope and an outshut in a continuous slope

Outshut – compartment at side or end of house or barn under a lean-to roof and not open to the body of the building

Gablet – small triangular gable at the top of a hip

Scantling – Measured size or dimensions of a timber

Scarf – Joint between two timbers meeting end to end

Skillet – Cooking pan with three feet and a long handle to stand over fire

Skimmer – Perforated utensil for skimming milk & other liquids

Spitter – Spade

Stop – Decorative end to a chamfer

Chamfer – Surface formed by cutting off a square edge at an angle

Trimmer – Short timber set across ends of rafters or joists to make an opening for a dormer or stair

Truss – A complete cross-frame from ground level to ridge in a box-framed or truck building

Closed truss – with the spaces between timbers filled in, as at the end of a building, between rooms and at the end of an open hall

Open truss – with spaces left open, as over a two-bay hall or in a barn

Weatherboarding – Wall cladding of overlapping horizontal boards

Wing – Part of house roofed at right angles to the main range

67 This is one of the Amberley houses where the stone walling contains a medieval timber-frame

Further Reading

Alcock N.W, Barley M.W., Dixon P.W., Meeson R.A. *Recording Timber-Framed Buildings: an illustrated glossary* (1996 CBA)

Bailey M. *The English Manor c1200–c1500* (2002, Manchester UP)

Beswick M. *Brickmaking in Sussex*, (1993, Middleton Press)

Birch R. *Sussex Stones: the story of Horsham Stone and Sussex Marble* (2006, Horsham)

Brown R.J. *Timber-Framed Buildings of England* (1990, Hale)

Bruce P. *Northchapel; A Parish History* (2000)

Brunskill R.W. *Traditional Buildings of England* (1992, Gollancz)
Brick Building in Britain (1990, Gollancz)

Cleere H. & Crossley D. *The Iron Industry of the Weald* (1985, Leicester UP)

Clifton-Taylor A. *The Pattern of English Building* (1980, Faber & Faber)

Dawson B. *Flint Buildings in West Sussex* (1998, West Sussex CC)

Harris R. *Discovering Timber-Framed Buildings* (1993, Shire Books)

Kenyon H. *The Glass Industry of the Weald* (1967, Leicester UP)

Lander, H. *House and Cottage interiors* (1982, Acanthus Books)

Mason, H.J. *Flint: the versatile stone* (2000, Providence Press)

Nairn, I. & Lloyd, D. *Hampshire* (Buildings of England, Penguin, 1967)

Nairn, I. & Pevsner, N. *Sussex* (Buildings of England, Penguin, 1965); in the course of revision

Mortimer, I. *The Time Traveller's Guide to Medieval England* (2009, Vintage)

Nash J. *Thatchers and Thatching* (1991, Batsford)

Quiney A. *The Traditional Buildings of England* (1990, Thomas & Hudson)

Rackham O. T*he History of the Countryside* (1987, Dent)
Trees & Woodland in the British Landscape (1998, Phoenix)

Roberts E. *Hampshire Houses 1250–1700* (2003, Hampshire CC)

Wight J. *Brick Building in England, from the Middle Ages to 1550* (1972, Baker)

68 The 'island' buildings in Midhurst's old market place, now The Swan, with its original jetty, and abutting double-jettied and gabled wing (left) with its unusual decorative framing. This once extended further north.

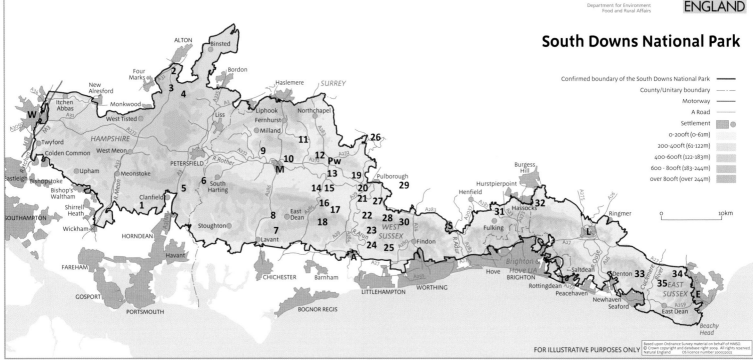

South Downs National Park

Confirmed boundary of the South Downs National Park
County/Unitary boundary
Motorway
A Road
Settlement
0-200ft (0-61m)
200-400ft (61-122m)
400-600ft (122-183m)
600 - 800ft (183-244m)
over 800ft (over 244m)

FOR ILLUSTRATIVE PURPOSES ONLY

Places within, or adjacent to, the South Downs National Park mentioned in the text or picture captions

W = Winchester	1 Hambledon	9 Woolbeding	17 Glatting	25 Bargham	32 DItchling
M = Midhurst	2 Chawton	10 Easeborne	18 Bignor	26 Wisborough	33 Alfriston
Pw = Petworth	3 Farringdon	11 Lurgashall	19 Fittleworth	Green	34 Polegate
A = Arundel	4 Selborne	12 Tillington	20 Hardham	27 Greatham	35 Filching
S = Steyning	5 Chalton	13 Byworth	21 Coldwaltham	28 Parham	
L = Lewes	6 Harting	14 Duncton	22 Amberley	29 Thakeham	
E = Eastbourne	7 Goodwood	15 Barlavington	23 Houghton	30 Sullington	
	8 Singleton	16 Sutton	24 Burpham	31 Poynings	

Places mentioned in text

(italicised names and/or numbers indicate illustrations)